Garden Answers Pruning

hamlyn

Garden Answers Pruning

Richard Bird

Expert answers to all your questions

A Pyramid Paperback from Hamlyn

First published in Great Britain in 2002
by Hamlyn,
a division of Octopus Publishing Group Limited,
2–4 Heron Quays,
London E14 4JP

This revised edition published in 2004

Distributed in the United States and Canada by
Sterling Publishing Co., Inc.
387 Park Avenue South, New York,
NY 10016-8810

ISBN 0 600 61024 1
EAN 9780600610243

A catalogue record for this book is available
from the British Library

Printed and bound in China
10 9 8 7 6 5 4 3 2

Contents

Introduction 6

Getting Started 8

Trees 18

Shrubs 30

Hedges and Topiary 48

Climbers 60

Roses 74

Tree Fruit 88

Soft Fruit 126

Troubleshooting 146

Glossary 152

Index 154

Acknowledgements 160

Introduction

***Helleborus orientalis* (Lenten rose)**

Pruning is one of those aspects of gardening that many gardeners would rather not have to do. It has a reputation for being a mysterious process that is not only complicated but also time consuming, and some gardeners are even rather frightened of it. This is probably because it involves cutting and removing part of a plant, which may be a problem if you are not really certain what you are aiming at or what the result will look like. Indeed, it is rather like cutting someone's hair: we are wary of trying it in case we cut off too much because we know that we can't put it back. So it is in the garden; the thought of cutting off too much from a particular plant deters people from undertaking any pruning at all.

Pruning is, however, nowhere near as difficult or complicated as many people imagine it to be. Nature is, in any case, often forgiving enough to allow us to try again the following year. Generations of gardeners have learned how to prune, largely by trial and error, and our gardens are filled with well-shaped trees, shrubs and climbers and productive fruit plants, all bearing witness to the fact that pruning is perfectly possible.

In almost every garden there are trees and shrubs that will look better and live longer if they are pruned. You can, of course, pay somebody to do it for you, but most gardeners are quite capable of carrying out all the pruning that is necessary. The key is to learn which plants need pruning and when and how to do it. This may seem daunting, but there are, in fact, only a limited number of types of pruning and only a few times in the year when plants should be pruned. The key is to know when and how to prune the different types of plant.

Rather than trying to learn every possible combination of plant type, pruning technique and timing, it is far easier if you concentrate on the individual plants that you already have in your garden. Knowing why you should prune a particular plant – to encourage flowering or fruiting shoots, to limit growth or to promote colourful leaves, for example – is the key to understanding when and how to prune any plant. Subsequently, you will be able to group the plants you have so that you tackle several at the same time and in more or less the same way. Then, whenever you add a new plant to your garden, all you need do is to check a few details about it – how and when it flowers, for example – and you can prune it as you do other, similar plants.

This book is intended to demystify pruning. Each chapter takes the form of a series of questions and answers, grouped by the main plant types, so that you can quickly find the information relevant to the different plants in your own garden. The pruning advice for an individual plant is accompanied by lists of some of the most popular plants that can be treated in a similar way. Even if a question does not refer specifically to a plant in your own garden, you will find that the advice can be applied to plants that you do have. Many of the pruning techniques are accompanied by step-by-step illustrations, to make the process even clearer.

Almond blossom

Rosa 'Climbing Iceberg'

Getting Started

Apple tree in flower

Why prune?

➡ Is pruning really necessary?

Most plants need to be pruned at one time or another. A tree or shrub may need pruning when it is first planted so that it can be trained into the shape you want, and this mainly involves the removal of unwanted branches and shoots. Mature plants may require annual pruning for a number of reasons. They may become overgrown, developing a tangled mass of stems going in all directions, many of them rubbing against each other. The thorns on an overgrown rose bush, for example, can cause a lot of damage in a strong wind. Regular pruning is an opportunity to remove dead and dying stems and branches, which not only makes the plant look neater but may also prevent disease from spreading to other parts of the plant. The process rejuvenates the plant, keeping it young so that it produces good foliage, flowers and fruit and generally stays looking attractive.

Many ornamental shrubs flower mainly or exclusively on young growth, and once branches are mature or old the number of flowers diminishes, while the size of the flowers borne on overgrown shrubs often also decreases. Shrubs grown for their foliage will usually have bigger and more intensely coloured foliage if the shrub is regularly pruned. Some shrubs are grown for the colour of the bark of the young wood, and this may be lost as the wood becomes older. The same problem of ageing wood may also apply to fruiting trees and bushes, which produce fewer and smaller crops on old wood. Finally, some plants are vigorous, and pruning is the only way to restrict their size, a factor which can be important in a small garden.

Reasons for pruning

Although most plants benefit from pruning at some stage in their life, the reasons for doing this vary from plant to plant. The most usual reasons are:

- Training and shaping
- Preventing plants from becoming overgrown
- Promoting flowers or fruit
- Encouraging the production of colourful leaves or bark
- Preventing disease and decay
- Rejuvenating plants
- Restricting size
- Creating special shapes (as in topiary)

➡ What is the first thing I should prune?

Although pruning requirements vary from plant to plant, certain types of wood regularly need attention. Dead, dying, diseased or damaged wood should always be a priority; not only does it disfigure a plant but it also fills up the interior, creating a tangle of branches that prevents air from circulating and light from penetrating. It can also harbour pests and diseases, which can possibly affect other parts of the plant.

Such branches should be removed: cut them right back to healthy wood. This will often open up the shrub or tree and allow you to look at it with a clearer eye so that you can see what to do next. Burn diseased wood rather than shredding it and adding it to a compost heap. Another type of wood that, although not dead, should be removed is suckers – these are new shoots growing from the base of a grafted tree or shrub.

➡ What should I cut out once I have removed the dead and diseased wood?

The next step is to see if there are any branches that cross through the plant, which will not only spoil the overall shape but also rub against other branches, causing wounds through which disease can enter the plant's tissue. Cut out the offending branches.

Trees and evergreen shrubs often need no further attention unless you want to alter their shape or reduce their size (see pages 21 and 34–5). Deciduous shrubs, however, often require additional pruning, and the next important task may be to remove some of the older growth so that the shrub is encouraged to produce new stems, which will rejuvenate the plant, enabling it to flower better. You may also need to remove the old flowered wood to promote new flowering wood (see Chapter 3, pages 30–47).

Finally, have a good look at the plant's overall shape to check that it has the typical form that might be expected from that type of plant, whether it is a shrub, tree or climber. Stray branches may be too long, or single branches might be sticking out at odd angles, and these should be removed or cut back.

➡ I have heard that if you cut certain types of plant back while they are in growth they will be shorter when they regrow. Is this true?

***Aster* × *frikartii* 'Mönch' (Michaelmas daisy)**

Yes. It is possible to restrict the height of some tall herbaceous plants by cutting them down after they have put on, say, 30cm (12in) of growth. The plants will start into growth again and, because they will try to bloom on time, will bear flowers lower down. This can be useful if your garden is exposed to strong winds or if you want a particular plant for its visual effect but would like it slightly shorter. Some forms of *Aster novi-belgii* (Michaelmas daisy) can be treated in this way, as can several taller plants, especially if they have a clump-forming habit of growth – *Sanguisorba officinalis* (great burnet), for example – but it is best to experiment with part of the plant first to see if it works before you cut down the whole plant.

What needs pruning

➡ Which plants need pruning?

***Chrysanthemum* 'Hunstanton'**

Most plants need pruning, even if it is only to cut them down when they are dead, but some plants require more care than others. On the whole, trees do not need much attention once they are beyond their formative stage, unless they have to be reduced in size. Shrubs and climbing plants need more pruning, and most species should be pruned at least once a year. Even within this group, however, there are many species, evergreens in particular, that need little regular pruning.

Many herbaceous plants need pruning, but they are tackled in a different way from shrubs. They are pruned either by deadheading (see pages 13–14), which promotes further flowering, or by cutting right back so that they produce new growth after they have finished flowering. Some plants, such as chrysanthemums, can be disbudded (see box, right) to concentrate growth into one or two flowers. At the end of the season, herbaceous plants are cut to the ground. Annuals (plants that grow from seed, flower and die within a single year) need cutting back to make them bush out and to remove any straggling growth as the season progresses. None of these plants is difficult to tackle, and the process soon becomes automatic.

➡ When should I cut the leaves off my daffodils?

Although the garden would look tidy if bulbs were treated in the same way as herbaceous plants and cut back as soon as the flowers were over (see pages 13–14), the bulb leaves are needed to produce food to be stored in the bulb for the following year. The foliage should, therefore, be left on all bulbs until it has started to yellow and wither, when it can be cut off.

The foliage of some bulbs, such as *Allium* spp. (ornamental onions), can look untidy even

***Narcissus* 'Jack Snipe'**

Disbudding

Gardeners who exhibit plants like chrysanthemums, dahlias and tuberous begonias strive to produce the best possible blooms, and size is often a factor. Disbudding is the process used to concentrate the plant's energy into a limited number of flowers. The young plant is stopped (see below right) to make it bush out. Later, some of the sideshoots are removed so that there are about four strong, healthy shoots on the main stem. As the flower buds begin to develop, the secondary sideshoots that have grown on the main sideshoots are removed so there is only one flower at the top of each shoot. Alternatively, the central bud at the tip of the main shoot is removed and the secondary sideshoots are allowed to produce flowers in order to get a spray of flowers.

when they are in flower. Even so, it should not be cut off because the bulbs must build up reserves for the following year, and cutting off the leaves too soon may even prevent them from flowering altogether. The best and easiest solution is to plant bulbs among other plants, such as deciduous shrubs and herbaceous perennials, which will hide the dying foliage as they come into growth themselves but allow the bulb flowers to be seen.

➡ Do ferns need pruning?

Ferns do not need to be pruned to shape them, but the dead fronds should be cut off. This is normally done in spring so that the old fronds give some frost protection to the crown of the plant. Do not remove the old leaves too late because you may damage the newly emerging fronds, which are usually particularly attractive.

Polystichum retrorsopaleaceum

➡ I have heard the word 'stopping' applied to plants. What does this mean?

Many plants, if allowed to develop naturally, would grow as a single stem with perhaps a solitary flower on top. Stopping or pruning the plant when it is young is a way of making it bush out and not only become a better, fuller shape but also flower more freely. Once the plant has started to grow away strongly, the tip is cut back to one or two pairs of good, strong leaves. This causes sideshoots to form. *Lathyrus odoratus* (sweet pea) and *Dianthus* cultivars (pinks) are good examples of this, but it applies to many plants that grow from a single basal stem.

Reasons to prune different plant types

Type of plant	Possible requirements
Ornamental trees (e.g. acer, magnolia, oak, sorbus)	Initial training Removal of dead wood
Fruit trees (e.g. apple, cherry, peach, pear)	Initial training Promotion of maximum fruiting
Evergreen shrubs (e.g. box, elaeagnus, euonymus, holly, rhododendron, skimmia, yew)	Initial training (optional) Removal of dead wood Shaping into hedge or topiary
Deciduous shrubs (e.g. buddleia, cornus, cotinus, deutzia, philadelphus, spiraea)	Initial training (optional) Removal of dead wood Removal of one-third of old material Promotion of the production of flowers, foliage or bark Trimming
Fruiting shrubs (e.g. blackberry, blackcurrant, blueberry, redcurrant)	Initial training Promotion of maximum fruiting
Climbers (e.g. clematis, honeysuckle, rose, wisteria)	Initial training Restriction of size Renewal of old wood
Hedges and topiary (e.g. beech, box, hawthorn, hornbeam, yew)	Initial training Removal of dead wood Keeping in shape
Herbaceous perennials (e.g. alchemilla, delphinium, geranium, lupin, poppy)	Promotion of new foliage and second flowering Deadheading
Annuals (e.g. calendula, lobelia, pelargonium, petunia)	Maintaining compact shape Deadheading

***Skimmia* 'Rubella'**

Annuals and herbaceous plants

Do annuals need pruning?

It may seem odd to prune annual plants, but they often benefit from it. At the early stages, many can be encouraged to bush out if the tip of the leading shoot (or 'leader') is removed. Other annuals, especially those used as bedding plants or in containers such as hanging baskets, have a long season, during which they produce a lot of flowers. This steadily weakens the plant, but if it is regularly deadheaded the energy-consuming seed production is curtailed and instead the energy is diverted into producing even more flowers.

As the season progresses, many plants become rather long and straggly, and they begin to look untidy, especially as the earlier leaves start to wither and die. Many stems can be cut back to a good bud so that replacement shoots develop, rejuvenating the plant. If this is done, many annuals will continue to produce flowers well into autumn. Cutting back in this way is particularly important for plants that are in containers, such as hanging baskets, windowboxes or tubs, where there is a limited amount of space and you do not want it filled with bare stems.

Do herbaceous plants need pruning?

Although pruning is generally regarded as something that is carried out only on woody subjects, such as trees or shrubs, if it is defined as cutting a plant to make it more productive or decorative, the cutting back of herbaceous and other perennial plants must count as pruning. Unless the plant is overgrowing its allotted position or has been damaged in some way, most of the pruning is done after flowering has finished. Deadheading and cutting back stems to promote new growth are the principal techniques.

Alchemilla mollis **(lady's mantle)**

Why do some gardeners cut herbaceous plants completely to the ground instead of deadheading them?

Some herbaceous plants flower over a relatively short period, and once their function is over they go into decline until they die back and retire underground until the next year. Between finishing flowering and dying back, there can be several months when the foliage looks tired and jaded, gradually becoming more tatty. If the whole plant is cut to the ground it will often put up new leaves, which will make an acceptable foliage plant for the rest of the season. *Alchemilla mollis* (lady's mantle) is one such well-known example. Sometimes, as well as producing new foliage, the plant will also produce a second flush of flowers, which would not happen if the plant were simply left to die down. *Nepeta* spp. (catmint) is an example of the type of plant that can be cut right back to the crown. When you remove all the foliage and stems, take care that you avoid any new foliage that may just be appearing.

➡ Is deadheading the same as pruning and how important is it?

Deadheading (the removal of dead flowers and flowerheads) is a form of pruning, but its importance and whether it should be carried out at all varies from plant to plant. There are two reasons for deadheading. The first is an aesthetic one: a plant covered with dead blooms looks untidy and, although some flowers go over relatively gracefully, others are extremely unattractive. White flowers turning brown, such as on a white lilac or white camellia, are particularly disfiguring.

The second reason for deadheading is a practical one: flowers usually die because they have been pollinated, and once this happens seeds or fruits begin to develop, a process that uses up a great deal of the plant's energy. If the old flowerheads are removed before they start to produce seed, a lot of energy is diverted into producing more flowers or new growth.

Deadheading usually involves cutting the stem at some point below the flower, preferably at a bud or leaf. Sometimes it is better to go further down the stem until you find a joint and remove it there, and there are times when it is much better to go right to the base of the plant and cut out the whole stem – daffodils, for example, look better if you do this. If a plant produces clusters of flowers, remove just the dead ones from the cluster until the last one dies, which you can cut at an appropriate place further down the stem.

Plants to cut back after flowering

The following herbaceous plants are among those that should be cut back after flowering. They generally produce a second display of foliage and may even bloom again.

- *Alchemilla mollis* (lady's mantle)
- *Delphinium* cultivars
- *Euphorbia amygdaloides* 'Purpurea' (wood spurge)
- *Geranium* spp. (not all)
- *Lamium* spp. (deadnettle)
- *Lupinus* cultivars (lupin)
- *Melissa officinalis* (bee balm)
- *Nepeta* spp. (catmint)
- *Papaver orientale* (oriental poppy)
- *Pulmonaria* spp. (lungwort)

Deadheading a rose

➡ There are several clumps of bamboo in my garden. How do I prune them?

Bamboos do not require regular pruning, and most species produce culms that live for anything between eight and ten years. Every spring, however, the dead culms should be removed from the base, although this is not always easy to do in real thickets. Cut the canes back to the ground or you will be left with ugly stumps. At the same time, to prevent the clumps from becoming too dense, you can remove some of the older canes.

When to prune

➡ When should I prune the plants in my garden?
Irritatingly, perhaps, there is no one time of year that will suit all plants. Some plants, including many trees and shrubs, are pruned in winter, during their dormancy, but exceptions include several popular members of the *Prunus* genus. Flowering cherries, for example are pruned in summer so that the cuts have time to heal before winter, while plants such as *Prunus lusitanica* (Portugal laurel) and *P. laurocerasus* (cherry laurel) are usually pruned in late spring or early summer.

Remember that you only need to know when to prune the plants in your own garden. Once you know the best time to prune them, it will soon become routine.

➡ I know that herbaceous plants die back each year, so why do they still need pruning?
If you do nothing, your herbaceous plants will grow up through the old dead stems and look rather messy. The normal procedure is to cut all dead growth right to the base once they have either started dying back or have turned brown. With plants such as Michaelmas daisies that have tough stems, make sure that you cut as low as possible; otherwise, each year you will need to cut higher and higher to avoid the previous year's dead stubs.

Some gardeners like to do this straightaway so that the garden is neat and tidy for winter and to save time in spring. Other people prefer to leave them until spring, either because they look attractive in winter when there is not much else to look at or because the stems carry seedheads, which provide food for birds. Insects overwinter in the base of the plant and in the seedheads, another good source of food for birds. Another reason for waiting until spring is

Helleborus orientalis **(Lenten rose)**

that the dead stems and foliage provide some protection for the crown of the plant from frost and from driving, compacting rain. If you delay cutting back until spring make sure that you cut everything down before the new growth starts, because cutting out dead stems from among the new ones can be awkward.

A number of perennials, such as hellebores and kniphofias, remain green during winter but produce new foliage in spring. Generally, the old leaves are not cut out until spring, just as the new ones are appearing. You could prune away the old leaves earlier, but the still-green foliage on these plants protects the crown and the new growth against frosts.

➡ Why can't I prune all the shrubs in my garden at the same time?
Life would certainly be easier if this was possible, but one of the great joys of having flowering shrubs is that they can provide colour and fragrance almost all year round. Most shrubs should be cut back after flowering, although some plants, such as fuchsias, flower continuously or late in the year, and they are often not pruned until the following spring.

Tools and equipment

➡ Which tools will I need to buy?

The most important tool you need is a good pair of secateurs. Always buy the best you can afford, because cheap secateurs often crush the wood rather than cutting it cleanly, allowing disease to enter the plant's tissues, and they also wear out quickly. Secateurs are available in a range of sizes, so try before you buy and get a pair that is comfortable to hold.

If you have hedges to cut, you will need shears, either hand- or power-operated, and hand shears are also ideal for clipping over annuals and plants such as heathers. Long-handled pruners, often called loppers, will make it easier to cut larger, tougher stems, especially if you do not have strong hands. Branch or tree loppers are ideal for removing shoots on tall trees; they are basically a pair of secateurs on a long handle, with a lever at the bottom.

At some stage you will also probably need a pruning saw. There are several types, but most gardeners use one of the folding models, which are efficient and easy to store. The blades are usually sharp but will eventually need replacing. A sharp knife is always useful around the garden, so you should have one anyway.

You will also find it useful to have a ladder or pair of steps if you have to prune climbers or trees. When you use ladders in the garden, make sure that someone can hold them steady while you work, or buy a stabilizer, which will prevent the ladder from toppling over. You will also need a pair of good-quality gardening gloves, especially when you are pruning thorny plants like roses, and if you use powered tools wear protective goggles and ear protectors.

Most garden tools are made to suit right-handed people; if you are left-handed and find conventional tools difficult to use, left-handed versions are available and are well worth searching out.

➡ What is the difference between anvil and bypass secateurs?

Anvil secateurs cut when a sharp, straight-edged blade cuts against a flat, firm surface (the anvil). Bypass secateurs (also known as curved or side-anvil) work like scissors, with a convex upper blade cutting against a concave or square lower blade. There is, in fact, a third type, parrot-beak secateurs, which also work like scissors but have two concavely curved blades; they are not suitable for stems more than about 1cm (½in) thick. As long as they are sharp and well maintained, all types can be used for pruning. Anvil secateurs, however, tend to crush the stem as they cut and are not, therefore, generally used for taking cuttings for propagating; they will, however, cut more reliably when they are slightly blunt.

➡ Are petrol-powered hedge-trimmers better than electric trimmers?

In terms of cutting power, there is little to choose between the two types. Petrol-powered trimmers are useful if the hedge to be cut is a long way from a power source, but it is also possible to have battery-operated, cordless trimmers, which will cut up to about 80 sq m (100 sq yd) of hedge between recharges. Although they are powerful, petrol trimmers are noisy and heavy.

Electric trimmers are generally easy to use and handle, but the main problem is the trailing cable. In the interests of safety, you should always install a circuit-breaking device just in case the cable is accidentally severed while you are working.

➡ What do I do with the prunings?

Until recently, prunings and hedge clippings were usually burned because they were too coarse to go on a compost heap. Shredders are now more widely available (and can be hired if you do not want to buy one), and prunings can

Tools and equipment

Over the years you will probably acquire the following tools to help you prune the range of trees, shrubs and other plants in your garden.

Anvil secateurs

Bypass secateurs

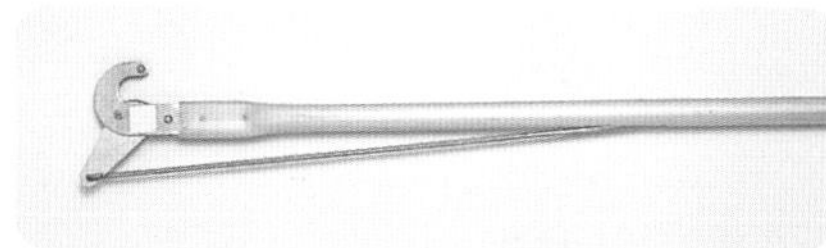

'Long arm' branch or tree loppers

Hedge-trimmer

Hand shears

Folding saw

be reduced to the consistency of chipped bark; after a couple of months of composting, they make an excellent mulch for borders and beds.

If you do not have hedges, or you have a small garden, you are unlikely to need a shredder. Some local authorities accept garden waste, which they use for compost making. You may have to take the bags of garden waste to the local refuse depot, but some authorities will collect it from you.

Some pruned material can be put to good use within the garden. Large, spreading branches or shoots can be used as sticks for supporting peas or flowering plants, or as temporary covers for seed beds to keep cats and birds from disturbing them.

Trees

Acer japonicum 'Vitifolium' (full-moon maple)

Basic techniques

How do I make pruning cuts?

Pruning cuts on stems and most slender branches are made with secateurs. Always cut back into sound wood – there is no point in cutting into dead or dying wood – and wherever possible cut back to an outward-facing bud – that is, a bud that is on the side of the stem away from the centre of the tree or shrub. This will make sure that the plant has an open structure and there is less crossing and tangled wood.

The cut should be made just above a bud. If a cut is made too close to a bud, it will damage it; if it is made too far away, the wood between

Good and bad pruning cuts

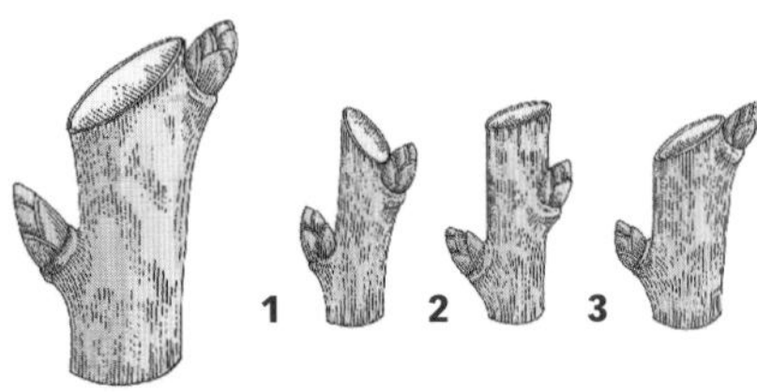

The first illustration (far left) shows the correct position of a pruning cut: the cut is slightly sloping, and the upper point is just above a bud. If the cut slopes down to a bud (**1**) there is a danger that it will be damaged. If it is too high (**2**) the stub may die back and lead to disease. If it is too close (**3**) the bud will be unsupported and damaged.

Pruning trees

Ideally, ornamental trees are pruned only to help the development of a straight, strong central stem and a shapely crown. In the early stages it may be necessary to remove low-growing branches, and occasionally a tree may develop a forked leading shoot, which will require some attention. Pruning to restrict size, however, should rarely be necessary and, if you find that you are continually having to cut back branches, it is most likely that you have planted the wrong type of tree for your garden.

the cut and the bud will die and could die back progressively, affecting the whole shoot. The cut should slope slightly away from the bud. Do not cut towards the bud. Finally, make sure that the cut is a clean one. Avoid crushing or tearing the wood or bark.

What is the best way to deal with thicker wood, such as branches?

The main problem with removing larger stems or branches is the weight that they carry. If you are not careful, as you cut through a branch its weight will suddenly make it break through the remaining wood, often tearing it well above the cut you are making. Apart from being ugly, this gash could allow disease in.

The best way of preventing this is to take the branch down in stages. First, cut off all the twigs and fine stems. Then make an upward cut from underneath the branch, about 30cm (12in) from its junction with the main trunk. Cut about one-third of the way through. Next, make a cut from above about 10cm (4in) further out along the branch from the upward cut. Continue until you either get right through the branch or it splits along to the undercut.

Once the branch has been removed, cut through the remaining stub of the branch close to the trunk, but not tightly up against it. Begin by cutting from below and finish the cut from above, making sure that the two cuts align and do not leave an uneven surface. Support the remains of the branch so that it does not fall in the final moments and tear the bark. When the final cut has been made, take a sharp knife and pare away the ragged bark around the cut so that it has a clean sloping finish with no snags through which diseases could possibly enter. See also Removing a large branch box, page 20.

What initial training do trees need?

When the tree is first planted, stake it well, and tie in the leader to make sure that it grows straight. Thereafter, there is little to do beyond ensuring that the shape is regular and even. This means making certain that it has only one leader. Carefully remove any competing shoot or shoots by pruning them out at the base, taking care not to damage the selected leader. You should also remove any misplaced branches or shoots, as well as any damaged or dead wood. As the tree grows, remove a few of the branches from the base, if necessary, to expose the trunk to the height you want.

Climbers to prune for renewal

The following climbers can be cut to the ground and will reshoot:

- *Campsis* × *tagliabuana*
- *Clematis* – some spp. and cultivars
- *Fallopia baldschuanica* (Russian vine)
- *Lonicera* spp. (honeysuckle) – some
- *Passiflora* spp. (passionflowers) – some
- *Solanum* spp. – some
- *Thunbergia* spp. (clock vine)

How much pruning is needed once the tree is mature?

Very little. Always keep an eye out for dead or diseased wood and remove it. Occasionally a branch will grow in the wrong direction – downwards, for example, when the natural habit is upwards – and this can have the effect of marring the overall appearance of the tree or make it look unbalanced. Such branches should be removed. Sometimes clusters of shoots (water shoots) appear on the trunk of a tree, either from the base or from knots where branches have previously been removed. If you notice these when they first appear, you can often rub them out with your thumb; otherwise, cut them off with secateurs.

Removing a large branch

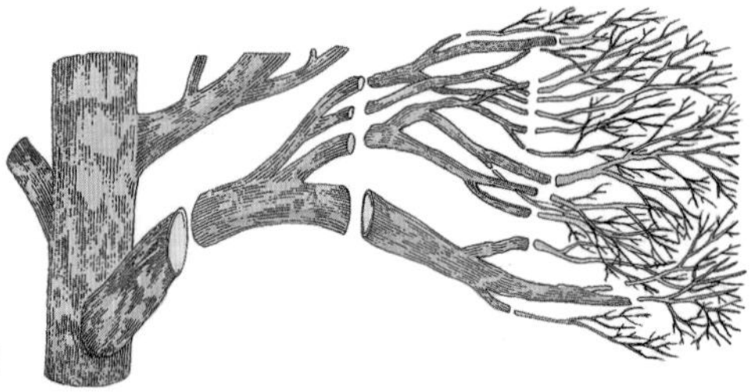

1

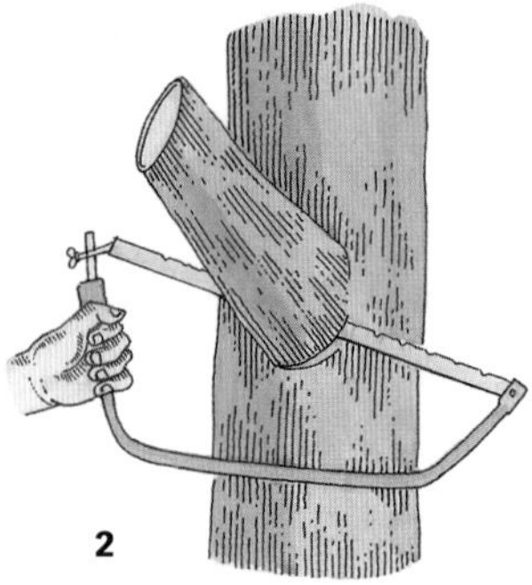

2

3

1 Remove large branches in sections. If you attempt to take an entire branch down with just a single cut, you may damage the tree.

2 Remove the final stump by sawing close to the main trunk. Begin by cutting up from beneath so that the stump does not fall and tear the bark.

3 Finish the cut from above, making sure that the two cuts align. Do not cut so close to the trunk that the bark is damaged by the saw.

4 Smooth the edges of the cut with a sharp knife. Edges that are jagged and bark that is torn will allow diseases and pests to gain a foothold.

5 When smooth, coat the site of the cut with a fungicidal wound paint.

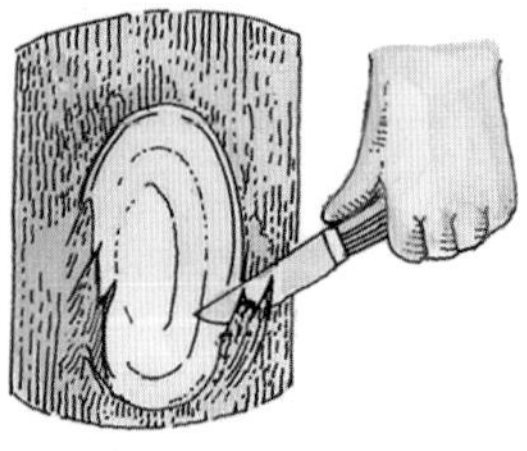

5

4

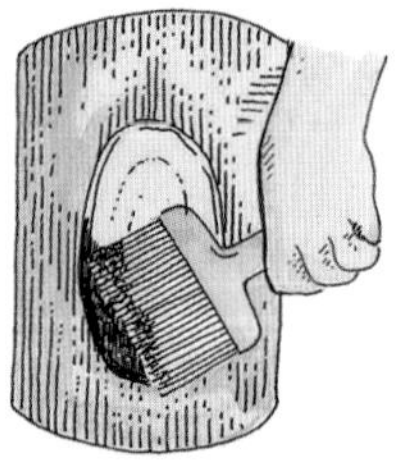

Pruning and removing trees

I have a tree that is getting too big for my garden. Can it be cut back?

Most trees look odd if they are heavily pruned, and they rarely recover their natural shape. Wherever possible, therefore, pruning established trees, except to remove dead and damaged branches, is best avoided. If you decide to go ahead with heavy pruning, the tree may look rather ugly for a number of years until it has regained its natural shape and appearance. The pruning itself should be undertaken over a number of years, especially if the tree is an old one, which might die if it is suddenly pruned hard. First, remove all dead, diseased or damaged wood (this should be done anyway, as a matter of routine) and also remove any branches that cross through the tree or rub against other branches. Then cut back all the branches to the desired size. In the following year, cut out any weak growth and reduce the number of new shoots to produce a balanced framework. Some trees can be shaped, even if it is not in a natural way – *Salix* spp. (willow), for example, can be pollarded (see pages 28–9).

If you have to reduce a tree in size, think carefully before you begin. It can be a big and dangerous job, and it is usually advisable to ask a qualified tree surgeon to do it. Make sure that any contractors you employ are properly qualified and are fully insured against any incidental damage.

I have had a large tree cut down but the base was left in the ground. How do I remove it?

Ideally, you should dig it out, but this can be a long and strenuous task, particularly if the stump has been cut low to the ground and it is difficult to get a leverage on the remains. One solution is to grind out the stump. Many tree surgeons will carry out this work with special equipment, which turns the stump into chippings that can be composted and used as mulch. It may be possible to hire such a machine if you want to do it yourself.

Oak tree stump

It is important to try to remove the stump, especially as it may bring honey fungus into the garden if it is left to rot down. If the tree is a type of *Crataegus* (hawthorn) it will regrow, first as a shrub and eventually into a tree. You could cut off any emerging shoots as you notice them and keep on until the stump loses strength and gives up. An alternative solution is to drill holes in the stump and fill them with a solution of ammonium sulphamate, which is obtainable from garden centres. You will not be able to plant in the nearby soil for about three months.

***Abies concolor* (white fir)**

Conifers

I have several coniferous trees in my garden. Are they all treated in the same way?

On the whole, yes, and generally they need no attention at all, apart from the removal of dead, dying, diseased and damaged wood. Sometimes it may be a good thing to clip lightly over a tree to keep it in perfect shape, but take care that you do not prune too deeply and cut into old wood because it will not recover. Sometimes a wayward branch will stick out and spoil the shape of an otherwise perfect conifer, and this can be cut off.

I planted a *Chamaeyparis lawsoniana* 'Ellwoodii' and it has developed two main stems. It seems perfectly healthy, so should I leave it alone?

Yes, this form of the lawson cypress will develop into a multi-stemmed tree. Most trees that develop two main stems do require attention, however, because the leaders will grow at angles and may eventually be pulled apart by the weight of the branches growing from them. Water can accumulate in the crack between the two leaders, leading to decay and rot, and in some instances part of the tree may simply be torn completely away, leaving an unattractively and potentially dangerous plant.

When should I prune the conifers in my garden?

If at all possible, do not prune your conifers at all, unless you have to remove dead or damaged branches. Although some conifers, such as *Chamaecyparis* and *Thuja*, will tolerate light clipping when they are young, only *Taxus* (yew) will regenerate from old wood, and if you

***Chamaecyparis lawsoniana* 'Aurea Erecta'**

accidentally cut into old wood you will be left with bare brown patches, which will never recover. Conifers that have been allowed to become overgrown can never satisfactorily be reduced in size or cut back. Conifers used for hedges (see pages 54–5) and topiary (see pages 58–9) can be cut back in early to mid-spring, with a second cut to maintain their shape done in late summer.

Small conifers

A tree that grows too large for its space will require constant trimming and pruning, which conifers don't like. Instead, if you have a small garden and want a reliable conifer for year-round structure and colour, select one of the following more compact forms.

- *Abies lasiocarpa* 'Arizonica Compacta' is a compact, slow-growing, conical tree, to 5m (15ft) tall, with bluish-grey leaves.
- *Calocedrus decurrens* (incense cedar) is a graceful, narrow, upright tree, to 5m (15ft) tall after 20 years (although ultimately larger), with bright green foliage.
- *Cedrus deodara* 'Aurea' (deodar) is a slow-growing, conical tree, to 5m (15ft) tall, with golden-yellow foliage that darkens to greenish-yellow in colour as the tree ages.
- *Chamaecyparis lawsoniana* 'Pygmaea Argentea', a slow-growing, rounded plant, grows ultimately to 2m (6ft) tall and is ideal for a container; it has white-tipped, bluish-green foliage.
- *Chamaecyparis obtusa* 'Nana Gracilis' is a slow-growing, pyramidal tree, eventually to 3m (10ft) tall, with gold-coloured foliage.
- *Cupressus sempervirens* 'Swane's Gold', a narrow, upright tree with golden foliage, will eventually get to 6m (20ft) tall but only to 1m (3ft) across; it is not reliably hardy.
- *Juniperus chinensis* 'Obelisk' is a slender shrub, to 2.5m (8ft) tall, with attractive blue-green to grey-green foliage.
- *Juniperus communis* 'Compressa', a slow-growing, dwarf plant, with greyish foliage, eventually gets to 1m (3ft) tall; it is ideal for rock gardens and containers.
- *Picea glauca* var. *albertiana* 'Conica' is a dwarf, cone-shaped shrub, with bushy but neat foliage.
- *Pinus mugo* 'Mops' (dwarf mountain pine), a dense, rounded bush, to 1m (3ft) tall, has bright green foliage.
- *Thuja orientalis* 'Aurea Nana' is a dwarf tree, to 60cm (2ft) tall, with yellow-green foliage, turning bronze in winter; ideal for growing in a container.
- *Thuja plicata* 'Hillieri', a dwarf, compact tree, to 3m (10ft) tall, this has blue-green foliage.

***Picea glauca* var. *albertiana* 'Conica'**

Eucalyptus gunnii (cider gum)

Evergreen trees

I thought that eucalyptus grew as evergreen trees, but I have seen a shrubby form. How is this pruned?

Most forms of eucalyptus do indeed grow as evergreen trees and as a rule need no pruning. Some species, however, notably *E. gunnii* (cider gum), have extremely attractive, bright blue-green juvenile foliage. The trees produce this attractive form of foliage only when they are young or when they are coppiced to keep them as a relatively small shrub. In its second spring, you can cut off a young tree at the base. This may seem drastic, but it will soon shoot from the base to form a bush of the desired foliage. Each spring, repeat the process, cutting the shoots to the ground and allowing new shoots to replace them. (See also Coppicing, page 28.)

What is the best way of training a bay tree as a standard?

Laurus nobilis (bay laurel) will grow into a fairly large tree if it is planted in a sheltered position, preferably protected from cold, drying winds. Eventually, plants can get to 6m (20ft) high and more. They are often grown as mophead standards in containers about 45cm (18in) across. Pruning and training, which takes several years, are best carried out in summer, so that the shoots have time to harden before cold winter weather arrives. Choose a plant with a strong leading shoot, and in the first summer remove the sideshoots to leave a clear stem. Allow the plant to grow up slightly higher than the ultimate height you want, but continue to remove the sideshoots. Encourage the shoots at the top to bush out by pinching out the growing tips; you should do this several times each summer. When the tree reaches the height you want, pinch out the top of the leading shoot.

Laurus nobilis (bay laurel)

Quercus rubra (red oak)

Deciduous trees

I have a large oak tree in my garden. How do I prune it?

There is very little for you to do, which is fortunate, because a mature, established oak tree can be a daunting prospect. Generally, you can leave the tree to its own devices, although it would be a good idea to cut out all dead wood. Even this, however, is mainly cosmetic because oak trees can live for years with branches that are completely dead. Cut them out if you can, but otherwise leave them as they are unless they might be dangerous. The only other thing you may want to do is remove some of the lower limbs to let in more light (see right). On a young oak it is worth removing double or multiple leading shoots to save yourself experiencing problems later on. All pruning of oaks should be carried out in winter, while the tree is dormant.

There is an established oak tree in my garden. It is dark under the tree, but I would like to be able to grow plants there. Is there anything I can do to increase the level of light?

It is possible to remove some of a tree's lower limbs and, done with care, it will not adversely affect the visual impact of the tree. Do not remove too many branches – just enough to allow more light in – and cut them off close to the trunk using the method described for large branches on page 20. Be careful not to overdo it and unbalance the shape of the tree.

This will increase the amount of light under the tree, but bear in mind that plants growing under trees have to compete with the tree for moisture and nutrients (and the tree will have an established root system), and also the ground under and immediately around a large tree is often drier than it is in the open garden, because the tree casts a rain-shadow. Removing some lower branches will do something to alleviate the dry conditions caused by the rain-shadow, but any plants grown under a tree will need additional water and nutrients if they are to grow satisfactorily.

I have a tree of heaven, which keeps producing shoots at some distance from the plant. What are these and should I remove them?

Ailanthus altissima **(tree of heaven)**

There are a number of shrubs and trees that behave in the same way as *Ailanthus altissima* (tree of heaven). The new growths are called suckers, and they appear from the roots of the plant. Sometimes suckers are produced when a tree's roots have been damaged. Some forms of *Prunus* (ornamental cherry trees) and *Populus* (poplar), for example, often have shallow roots and these frequently spread just below the surface of the lawn. If they are caught and wounded by the lawnmower suckers are likely to appear at those places.

The suckers should be removed, because they all have the potential of growing into a tree themselves. The normal way to remove them is to cut them off as close to the root as possible, which will mean digging down to the point at which the sucker has developed from the root. If you cut them off at ground level, several other shoots will grow to replace the one you have cut off. Some gardeners advocate tearing the sucker from the root, others making a clean cut. If you want a new plant, pot up the suckers (instead of taking root cuttings) in winter.

I have a lime tree and there are masses of small shoots appearing from the trunk. What are they and what should I do about them?

The shoots appearing on your *Tilia* (lime) are quite normal: they are just suckering growth. They can be simply cut off flush with the trunk of the tree with your secateurs. Do this every year to keep the trunk clear.

Should I remove the ivy that is growing around the trunk of several trees in my garden?

Many gardeners like to remove ivy in the belief that it will 'strangle' a tree. In fact, ivy often gets established only under and around a tree that is already dead or that is old or not entirely healthy. The dense shade cast by the canopy of a healthy tree will often prevent ivy from getting established. Because of its value as shelter for wildlife, leave ivy unless you have planted the tree especially for the appearance of its trunk.

Do I need to prune my silver birch?

Apart from the regular removal of dead and diseased wood, *Betula pendula* (silver birch) needs no special attention. Crossing branches that have to be removed should be cut out in summer to prevent sap from bleeding; but, on the whole, trying to shape the tree otherwise would upset its shape and it would be unlikely to recover. If the tree has outgrown its space, the best thing would be to remove it and start

Weeping trees

The following are just a few of the trees that will make a graceful, weeping feature tree. None of them needs pruning to achieve a natural, weeping shape.

- *Alnus incana* 'Pendula' (grey alder)
- *Betula pendula* (silver birch); *B. pendula* 'Tristis'; *B. pendula* 'Youngii' (Young's weeping birch)
- *Cercidiphyllum japonicum* f. *pendulum* (katsura tree)
- *Chamaecyparis nootkatensis* 'Pendula' (nootka cypress)
- *Fagus sylvatica* 'Pendula' (weeping beech)
- *Fraxinus excelsior* 'Pendula' (weeping ash)
- *Ilex aquifolium* 'Pendula'
- *Pyrus salicifolia* 'Pendula'
- *Quercus robur* f. *pendula*
- *Salix caprea* 'Kilmarnock'; *S.* 'Erythroflexuosa'

again. They are fast-growing plants and will soon fill the gap removing one will leave.

I have bought an *Amelanchier lamarckii*, but it has several stems rising from the base. I thought I was buying a tree. What should I do?

Some trees can exist in two forms: as a tree with a single trunk or as a shrubby tree with several (or many) main stems growing from the base. This amelanchier is one; *Corylus* (hazel) and *Prunus* × *subhirtella* (winter cherry) are others. Although it is easier if you buy one that is already trained as a one-trunk tree, you can train it yourself by selecting the strongest of the stems and removing all others at the base. Remove any that regrow and trim off any of the lower sideshoots from the main stem so that it develops into a trunk.

Amelanchier **(showing suckers)**

How do I prune a weeping tree?

Salix caprea **var.** ***Pendula***

There is no difference in pruning a weeping tree and pruning an ordinary tree. It is just a matter of removing any dead or damaged wood and cutting out any misplaced shoots, and with larger trees, such as tall weeping willows or weeping birches, even this is unnecessary. Smaller, grafted trees need more attention, because, for example, upward-growing stems will show up and should be removed. These smaller trees often grow like umbrellas, with a cascade of branches developing from the crown of the tree. If sideshoots develop on the trunk, they should be removed.

Coppicing, pollarding and pleaching

What is coppicing?

Coppicing is the cutting back to ground level of a tree to encourage the growth of several new stems from a single rootstock. It is usually carried out in late winter or early spring. Some trees – *Castanea sativa* (sweet chestnut), *Fraxinus* spp. (ash) and *Corylus* spp. (hazel) are the most common examples – are regularly cut to the ground. If they are left to their own devices, they grow into standard trees, often tall and gnarled when they get old. However, if they are cut back to the ground they produce new shoots from which young trees will grow. Coppicing can, therefore, be used as a method of keeping trees small, but it is a practice traditionally used to produce a steady crop of timber. The new shoots are allowed to grow for a number of years, depending on the soil and growth rate of the tree, but usually for between seven and 14 years. At this stage the trunks are still straight, and when they are cut they make good poles with a wide range of uses.

Is pollarding the same as coppicing?

No, not exactly. Pollarding, which is also carried out in late winter or early spring, involves cutting back the branches of a tree to the trunk to promote the production of young shoots. When the trunk reaches the desired height above ground, the leader is cut off and branches are allowed to develop from this point. These branches are removed regularly, once a year or, at most, every two years, so that new shoots are constantly produced.
In the past it was a method of producing wood for, among other things, kindling. In most cases the trees could have been coppiced – that is, cut off at ground level – but browsing animals would have prevented the shoots from

Trees that are suitable for:

Pleaching

- *Carpinus betulus* (hornbeam)
- *Tilia × euchlora*
- *Tilia platyphyllos*

Coppicing

- *Castanea sativa* (sweet chestnut)
- *Cornus alba* (red-barked dogwood); *C. stolonifera* 'Flaviramea'
- *Corylus avellana* (hazel)
- *Eucalyptus globulus* (Tasmanian blue gum); *E. gunnii* (cider gum)
- *Fraxinus* spp. (ash)
- *Salix alba* subsp. *vitellina* (golden willow); *S. alba* subsp. *vitellina* 'Britzensis'; *S. fargesii; S. irrorata*

Pollarding

- *Acer pensylvanicum* 'Erythrocladum' (snake-bark maple)
- *Eucalyptus pauciflora* (cabbage gum, weeping gum)
- *Populus × canadensis* 'Aurea'; *P. × jackii* 'Aurora'
- *Salix acutifolia* 'Blue Streak'; *S. daphnoides* 'Aglaia'; *S.* 'Erythroflexuosa'
- *Tilia platyphyllos* cultivars (large-leaved lime)

growing. Allowing the new stems to emerge from the top of the trunk meant that they were out of reach of such animals. Although the method is still used commercially to produce willow, it is not much used otherwise except in a decorative way. Some trees – *Tilia* spp. (lime), for example – are pollarded to keep their size under control. Such methods are popular with local authorities along urban streets. Pollarding can also be used in gardens to create attractive avenues, and it can be adopted in smaller gardens where the idea of larger trees is attractive but there is insufficient space to allow them to grow to full size. It can also be used to produce 'mophead' trees.

What are linked rows of trees called?

You are thinking of pleached trees, which are pruned and trained in such a way that the branches reach out horizontally and link up with the horizontal branches of the adjacent tree to create a 'wall'. The trunks are usually (but not always) kept clear of branches so that the finished effect resembles a floating hedge. They are usually arranged in rows, but sometimes in circles or curves. Pleached trees are also trained in a horizontal plane to form a 'roof'. Using this technique it is possible to create a completely green room, with all four sides and the ceiling composed of branches covered with green leaves. Occasionally they are only trained in a horizontal plane to create a shady area for sitting.

How do I create pleached trees?

You will need a framework of stout poles set about 2.5m (8ft) apart and linked by wires or battens of wood nailed to the uprights at distances of about 60cm (2ft), starting at 1.2m (4ft) or whatever height you want the branches to start. At each pole, plant a young tree. Tie in two suitable branches along the lowest wire. Remove any other sideshoots as well as any further sideshoots on those that you have just tied in. In subsequent years, as the trees grow, tie in appropriate sideshoots along the higher wires, removing all other sideshoots. When the top is reached, cut back the leader to the level of the topmost horizontal. Prune back any sideshoots produced on the horizontal branches to two or three buds. Remove any that grow out sideways. The idea is to create a narrow, vertical wall of stems and foliage. When the main stems meet along the wires, allow them to intertwine for a short distance before cutting out the tips. Once the horizontal branches have matured and are firmly in place, remove the framework. Do not allow any new shoots to develop on the trunks.

Pleached *Carpinus* (hornbeam) tunnel

Shrubs

General maintenance

I have just moved into a new house with several shrubs in my garden. How do I prune them?

This depends on what they are: each type of shrub has its own requirements and should be pruned at different times. This sounds rather daunting, but there is only a limited number of categories, each with its own procedures, which can be quickly learned. If you do not know the names of the shrubs, do nothing for the first year except to remove dead, damaged or diseased stems. As you notice when they flower or what type of growth they make, you will begin to understand when and how they need to be pruned. If it is your first experience of pruning, do not worry: even if you make a few mistakes you are unlikely to kill the shrubs, and they will generally regrow to allow you to try again.

Are there any shrubs that can be cut back to the ground?

Some overgrown deciduous shrubs that produce flowers on new wood will respond well to being cut right back to the ground or, at least, to being cut hard back (see page 43). They will usually reshoot and form a new bush. This treatment is appropriate only when they are overgrown or have outgrown their allotted space, however, and in normal circumstances they are treated as appropriate for their pruning

Viburnum tinus (laurustinus)

Shrubs to rejuvenate

The following evergreen and deciduous shrubs can be cut hard back to rejuvenate them. When you have cut back the branches almost to ground level, remember to apply a mulch of well-rotted compost or manure around the base.

- *Aucuba japonica* (spotted laurel)
- *Berberis* spp.
- *Corylus* avellana (hazel)
- *Crataegus* spp. (hawthorn)
- *Elaeagnus* spp.
- *Forsythia* spp.
- *Gaultheria mucronata*
- *Hebe* cultivars (most)
- *Olearia* × *haastii* (daisy bush)
- *Philadelphus* spp. (mock orange)
- *Prunus laurocerasus* (cherry laurel); *P. lusitanica* (Portugal laurel)
- *Rhododendron ponticum*
- *Viburnum tinus* (laurustinus)
- *Weigela* spp.

group. Be careful, however, because not all shrubs will tolerate such drastic action and there is a chance they may never recover. Some evergreen shrubs also respond well to being cut hard back (see pages 34–5).

Can anything be done to renovate an overgrown shrub?

Some shrubs are easy to deal with: they can be rejuvenated by cutting them to the ground (see left). With others, however, a more restrained approach is required. With these shrubs it is better to renew them over a period of about three years. Each year, cut out one-third of the old wood right to the ground while you prune the rest of the bush as normal. Also remove any misplaced branches that cross through the bush and any branches that rub against others. This will eventually rejuvenate the whole shrub, and from this point it is important to follow a regular pruning regime so that it does not become overgrown again. If the severe pruning stimulates a great number of new shoots, reduce them to an acceptable number to prevent them from overcrowding the bush. Some shrubs, including evergreen forms of ceanothus, will not regenerate from old wood and there is little you can satisfactorily do except dig up the plant and start again.

How should I tackle the *Kerria japonica* in my garden, which does not seem to grow in the same way as other shrubs and bushes?

The stems of most shrubs grow from more or less one place, but the deciduous *Kerria japonica* is a suckering shrub, which sends up the rather graceful, arching shoots from below ground. After flowering, cut out all the dead, dying and diseased wood as usual. If the kerria is outgrowing its allotted space, prune back about one-third of the stems, taking out the older and weaker stems first and cutting them back to 5cm (2in) or so above ground level, just

Kerria japonica

above a strong bud. Reduce the length of the remaining stems by between two-thirds and a half, once again cutting back to a strong, vigorous sideshoot.

If the suckers are spreading too quickly and the bush is becoming too large, dig round the central core and remove excess suckers from below ground.

Are there any shrubs that I can buy that need no pruning?

Most shrubs benefit from at least some pruning, even if it is just the removal of dead or damaged wood and most need pruning to perform at their best. That said, a number can be more or less left to their own devices. Conifers are probably the best examples, while many evergreen shrubs and a lot of miniature shrubs grown on rock gardens rarely need attention. Some ordinary garden shrubs, although they are better if pruned, can be left; the shrubby potentillas, *Potentilla fruticosa* and its cultivars and hybrids are good examples.

Evergreen shrubs

What should I do with the evergreen shrubs in my borders?

Although there are a few exceptions, evergreen shrubs generally need little pruning. That is not to say, however, that you need do nothing at all. As with all plants, dead, dying, diseased or damaged wood should be removed, making sure you cut back into healthy wood. There are some evergreen shrubs – camellias, for example, (especially white ones) – which will look better if the dead flowers are removed (see pages 13–14). This sort of pruning should be carried out in late winter or early spring.

An evergreen shrub may occasionally throw out a wayward shoot – one that is too large or sticks out in the wrong place – and this should be removed. Sometimes a variegated evergreen may produce leaves that are green rather than variegated – a characteristic known as reversion (see right). Any stems that have reverted should be completely cut out, otherwise there is a danger they will overcrowd the rest of the foliage. The box below lists varieties of evergreen shrubs that are particularly susceptible to reverting.

I have heard that mahonia can be grown as groundcover. How is it that this is possible?

Only *Mahonia aquifolium* (Oregon grape), which is comparatively low-growing, is suitable; *M. aquifolium* 'Apollo' is especially useful in creating a dense thicket of growth. Cut plants hard back in spring.

Other forms of mahonia are more upright and are more valued for their yellow flowers in late winter and spring. In general, mahonias need little pruning, although they can be pruned hard if they become leggy or if they outgrow their space. Any weak or dead stems can be cut out in spring, and frost-damaged shoots should be removed at the same time. Unwanted suckers should be removed at any time between late autumn and early spring.

I have an *Elaeagnus pungens* 'Maculata', which I planted for its gold and green variegated leaves, but I notice that some of the branches are bearing plain green leaves. What has happened?

The problem is known as reversion, and it often happens to variegated plants. Many cultivars that have variegated foliage originated as an

***Ilex* × *altaclerensis* 'Golden King' (holly)**

Reversion

The following plants are particularly prone to reverting:

- *Acer negundo* 'Variegatum'
- *Acer platanoides* 'Drummondii'
- *Elaeagnus pungens* 'Maculata'
- *Euonymus fortunei* 'Emerald 'n' Gold'
- *Ilex* cultivars (holly)
- *Pieris japonica* 'Variegata'
- *Spiraea japonica* 'Goldflame'

Elaeagnus pungens **'Maculata'**

Corylus avellana **'Contorta' (corkscrew hazel)**

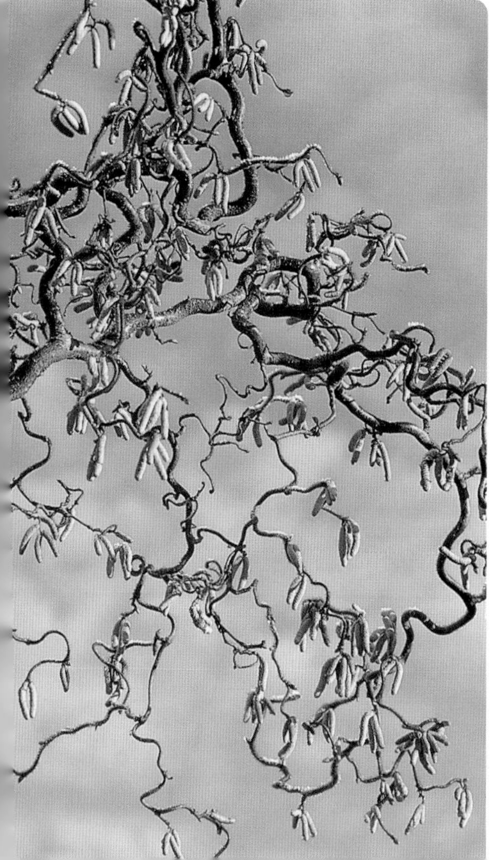

accidental shoot on an otherwise normal, all-green plant. The shoot would have been grown on into an all-variegated plant from which further plants could be propagated. Occasionally, these plants throw up a shoot of their original all-green foliage. When this occurs, it is important to prune it out completely, or the whole bush may eventually turn back to green. Shoots bearing all-green leaves are more vigorous than shoots bearing variegated leaves because the all-green leaves produce more chlorophyll. Cut the shoot out back to the main stem or, if that is not possible, to a stem carrying variegated leaves, and keep an eye out for any more that may occur.

A similar problem can arise on plants grown for their attractively twisted stems – *Corylus avellana* 'Contorta' (corkscrew hazel) or *Salix babylonica* var. *pekinensis* 'Tortuosa' (dragon's claw willow), for example – when straight stems are produced. Once again, these should be cut out as close as possible to the main stem as soon as they are noticed.

If evergreens need little pruning, why are plants such as holly and yew used as hedges that need trimming?

The general rule of not pruning evergreens holds not because shrubs will die if pruned, but rather because it is not strictly necessary to do so. In many cases, the shrubs will look better if left, especially if grown for their foliage rather than for their flowers (pruning is often used as an aid to flowering).

Many evergreens can be pruned quite hard: spotted laurel (*Aucuba japonica*), for example, can be cut right back to the ground. Conifers are an exception to this rule; although yew can be hard pruned, most other conifers are best with only a light trim of new growth as cutting into old wood can be fatal.

Aucuba japonica 'Crotonifolia' (spotted laurel)

Large-leaved evergreen shrubs

I have a spotted laurel that dominates a small border. I like the glossy leaves and would be sorry to lose it. Can I cut it back or should I replace it completely?

Evergreen shrubs like *Aucuba japonica* (spotted laurel), and its many attractively variegated cultivars, can be rejuvenated if they are cut back in spring. All the stems should be back to about 30cm (12in) above ground level. Plants which are extremely old and overgrown should be cut back so that the branches are about 60cm (2ft) long. You will probably need to use strong, double-action loppers, or possibly a pruning saw, to cut through the thickest stems. After pruning, dig in a mulch of well-rotted compost or manure around the plant.

I have an established *Rhododendron* 'Kilimanjaro' in my garden, but it has become rather leggy. How should I prune it?

As a general rule, rhododendrons do not need regular pruning, but when they get straggly and overgrown, they can be cut back. *R.* 'Kilimanjaro' is a vigorous plant, which can get to 2.1m (7ft) high and across, and it can look rather untidy if left unpruned. Unlike the species rhododendrons, hardy cultivars like this that have become overgrown can be cut back hard, a process that is best carried out over three years.

In mid-spring, cut back about one-third of the main stems to 30–45cm (12–18in) long, cutting back into healthy, strong wood. At the same time, prune out any dead or damaged stems. Repeat the process on the remaining stems in subsequent years.

Pruning rhododendrons

Strongly growing rhododendrons, which may need to be cut hard back every seven to ten years, include: 'Corry Koster', 'General Eisenhower', 'John Waterer', 'Louis Pasteur', 'Marchioness of Lansdowne', 'Moser's Maroon' and 'Professor J.H. Zaayer'. Not all rhododendrons will respond to being pruned, and they do not always make new shoots from old wood; this group includes cultivars in the Nobleanum Group and 'Alice', 'Bagshot Ruby' and 'Mrs C.B. van Nes'.

Rhododendrons should not be pruned unless they are growing strongly and are healthy, and not before they are at least three years old. All rhododendrons benefit from deadheading, although this is not always possible on large plants.

I planted a *Camellia japonica* a year ago. Should I be pruning it?

Camellia japonica **'Desire' (common camellia)**

Yes, if you wish. Many camellias are left unpruned, apart from the removal of winter-damaged shoots in late spring, and of dead or diseased shoots whenever they are noticed. Such camellias will make large, rounded shrubs. However, annual pruning immediately after flowering will keep the plant compact and bushy; plants can be deadheaded at the same time. Overgrown camellias can be pruned hard back, if desired, immediately after flowering.

Winter damage

In spring, use sharp secateurs to cut back large-leaved evergreen shrubs if the leaves have been damaged by frost.

Rejuvenating shrubs

An overgrown evergreen shrub such as *Aucuba japonica* can be cut hard back in spring. It will soon produce new shoots from the base.

Flowering evergreen shrubs

Santolina chamaecyparissus *(cotton lavender)*

I love the blue flowers of ceanothus but I am told they are difficult to grow. How should they be pruned?

There are two types of ceanothus, deciduous and evergreen species, and they are not reliably hardy, which may explain their reputation as difficult plants. The evergreen species that flower in spring to early summer include *Ceanothus arboreus, C. dentatus, C. impressus* and *C. rigidus*, and many fine cultivars have been developed from these species. All spring- and early-summer-flowering evergreen ceanothus that are grown as free-standing shrubs can be pruned after the flowers have faded; cut back the current year's growth to 2–3cm (about 1in) from the previous year's wood. Some evergreen ceanothus, including the popular 'Autumnal Blue', flower in summer to early autumn; they should be pruned in spring, before the plants start into growth again, by cutting back the stems that developed in the previous year to about half their length. During pruning of both types, remove any long, overgrown shoots to keep plants neat and compact. Ceanothus are often grown as wall shrubs (see pages 46–7).

I notice that santolina gets straggly if left unpruned. What is the best way to tackle it?

Santolina chamaecyparissus (cotton lavender) should be treated in much the same way as you would treat lavender (see below). You can remove the flowerheads by lightly clipping them off with shears as they go over in late summer, but you should leave the main pruning until spring, when the new growth is starting, because the plant is likely to die if it is pruned in autumn. Cut the shoots back by about half, to maintain a neat, compact shape, but take care that you do not cut into the old wood as it will not rejuvenate. It is true that these plants can become straggly and unattractive if they are left unpruned.

I know that lavender is classified as an evergreen shrub. Should it be left unpruned?

Lavender is an evergreen shrub, but it is an exception to the general rule in that it does need annual pruning. Some gardeners prune it in two stages; others prefer to do it in one go. The two-stage method is to remove the flower spikes once the flowers are dead by cutting

Pruning lavender

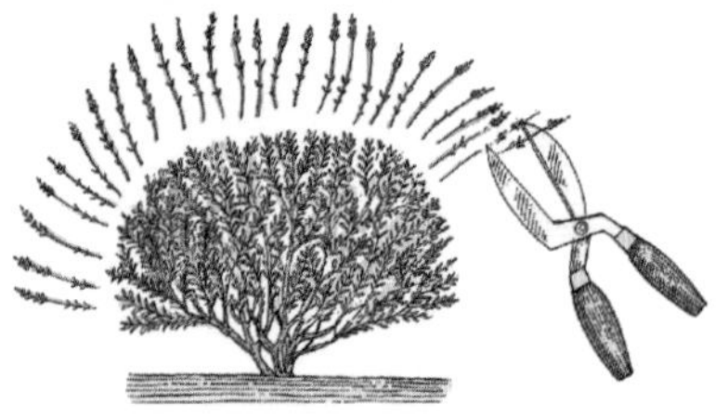

Lavender flowers can be easily removed in late summer or early autumn with a pair of hand shears. Wait until the following spring before cutting into the leafy shoots.

them off with garden shears; if you want to dry the flowers, cut them off soon after they open. The bush is then given a trim in spring, when 2–3cm (about 1in) of the previous year's growth is cut out. Take care that you do not cut back into the older wood: you can identify the previous year's growth because it will still be green and pliable. Trim the bush so that it has a rounded profile. Doing this each spring will help to ensure that the bush stays compact and shapely.

The alternative method is to leave the flowerheads on until the following spring and to remove both the flowerheads and some of the previous year's wood at the same time.

Lavender can become leggy and overgrown if it is not trimmed regularly, and forms of *Lavandula angustifolia* often get woody and unattractive at the base. Such plants should be replaced every eight to ten years.

Are winter- and summer-flowering heathers treated in the same way?

Erica tetralix **(cross-leaved heather)**

No, not exactly. Trim callunas and summer-flowering ericas in spring, clipping off the dead flowers and creating a neat, smooth outline. Take care that you do not cut into the young shoots, because these will bear the flowers later in the year. You should trim winter- and spring-flowering ericas as soon as the flowers have gone over. Daboecias should be pruned in late autumn, after flowering, although in cold areas this pruning should be left until spring because any young shoots that develop after pruning might be killed by winter frost.

Trimming heather

Use hand shears to prune heathers so that you can create a neat, smooth outline.

The hebes in my garden are looking straggly and overgrown. When should I cut them back?

Most larger, flowering hebes continue to grow and will become straggly and unattractive if left unattended. Many of the smaller ones, and so-called whipcords, usually retain their shape and need little attention apart from removing straggly or misplaced stems. Larger hebes should be clipped over immediately after flowering, pruning back to buds or new growth. Many continue flowering throughout the year so the best time to do this is in early autumn after the main flush of flowers. Pruning can be left until the spring, but this means that the shrub will not flower that year. Hebes that have a main flush in autumn or winter should be pruned in spring. If annual pruning has been ignored and the plant has become leggy, cut out up to one-third of the old growth to a strong bud or young shoot in the spring for three years in a row.

Physocarpus opulifolius **'Dart's Gold'**

Deciduous shrubs

I am about to plant a *Physocarpus opulifolius* 'Dart's Gold'. Should I prune it straight away?

This attractive deciduous plant will develop into a compact, suckering shrub, with bright yellow young foliage. Many shrubs are in perfect condition when you buy or receive them and so need little or no attention. However, you should check carefully, because some plants are not particularly well prepared for planting and may need a bit of pruning.

First, remove any dead or broken shoots. In addition, cut out any stems that cross each other, especially in the middle of the plant and if they are rubbing against other shoots. Finally, remove any unnaturally long or weak shoots. Aim for a balanced framework from which a good shrub will subsequently develop.

Although it is not directly connected with pruning, it is important to consider staking newly planted shrubs if they are in exposed positions. The stake should be put in position before the shrub is planted so that it is not driven through the unseen roots below ground. Only a short stake is needed and the main stem of the shrub should be firmly fixed to it using a proper tree tie. It should be no more than 30cm (12in) above the ground and should be checked regularly, and slackened if necessary, to ensure that it does not bite or chafe into the bark.

Do deciduous shrubs need any pruning before they reach maturity?

Usually, they will need pruning only to ensure that they are growing to the correct shape. Remove overlong and weak shoots. Shrubs such as *Physocarpus opulifolius* are generally pruned between late autumn and early spring, which is during the plant's dormancy. If you want to be able to plant under a shrub, you may want to remove some of the lower branches as the upper ones develop and take over development of the shrub.

➡ Are all deciduous shrubs pruned in the same way?

No, they are not. There are several options, ranging from no action at all to cutting the plant almost to the ground. Many deciduous shrubs need little or no pruning, but those that flower on old wood and those that are grown for their decorative foliage or bark, need special attention. Shrubs may also need to be pruned if they are damaged by winter frosts or snow or if they show signs of reversion or die-back.

Pruning deciduous shrubs

Rather than worrying about whether you should be pruning the shrubs in your garden, bear in mind that most require little or no pruning at all. Apart from the removal of dead or diseased wood, the following deciduous plants can be left pretty well to their own devices: *Acer* spp. (maple); *Amelanchier* spp. (serviceberry); *Arbutus* spp. (strawberry tree); *Buddleja globosa* (orange ball tree); *Colutea* spp.; *Cornus alternifolia* (green osier), *C. kousa*; *Corylopsis* spp. (winter hazel); *Daphne* spp.; *Fothergilla* spp.; *Hibiscus syriacus* (mallow); *Magnolia* spp.; *Potentilla fruticosa* and cultivars (shrubby cinquefoil); *Rhus typhina* (staghorn sumach); *Styrax* spp. (snowbell); *Syringa* spp. (lilac); and *Viburnum* spp.

***Arbutus unedo* (strawberry tree)**

Winter-flowering deciduous shrubs

When is the best time to prune a witch hazel?

Hamamelis spp. (witch hazel) bear fragrant, spidery-looking, yellow flowers on bare stems in winter to early spring, and in autumn the mid-green leaves turn a warm golden-yellow before falling. Apart from removing dead or damaged wood, which should be done in late winter or early spring, these plants need no regular pruning. If necessary, cut out straggly or overcrowded stems in early spring.

Hamamelis mollis **(Chinese witch hazel)**

Do winter-flowering deciduous shrubs need pruning at all?

These shrubs need little attention. Some benefit from shaping when they are first planted (see pages 38–9), and as with all shrubs it is important to remove any branches that cross the plant's centre, which causes congestion and reduces the amount of light and air that can reach the central stems, thereby inhibiting the ripening and maturing of the wood. Always remove any shoots that have been damaged by pests or diseases; if these are left on the plant, they lead to decay and may infect other parts of that and other, nearby plants.

Prune winter-flowering shrubs as soon as the flower display is over. This will give the plant the maximum amount of time to produce new shoots, which will be able to ripen before the onset of cold winter weather. It is easier to control the size of winter-flowering plants than almost any other type of plant.

Removing damaged wood

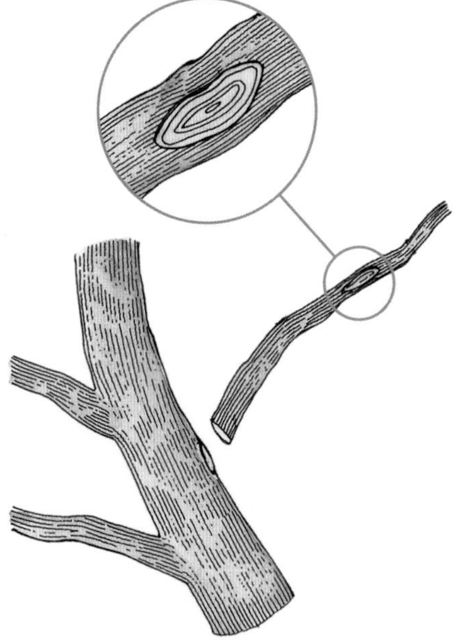

Cut out damaged shoots of winter-flowering deciduous shrubs at their base in spring.

Weigela florida 'Foliis Purpureis'

Early-flowering deciduous shrubs

What is the best way to tackle shrubs that flower early in the year, between late spring and midsummer?

Early-flowering deciduous shrubs, such as *Weigela florida* 'Foliis Purpureis', should, like early-flowering shrubs, be pruned as soon as their flowers fade. The difference is, of course, that the pruning is done several months later.

First, cut out all thin, weak shoots and any that cross in the centre of the plant. Next, cut back to within two or three buds from the base all those shoots that have borne flowers. The remaining young shoots will bear the flowers the following year. This treatment encourages the production of fewer, but larger, flowers.

Neglected and overgrown shrubs can be rejuvenated by cutting them right back, almost to ground level, but this drastic treatment usually means that they do not produce flowers for at least one season.

How should I prune a *Magnolia stellata*?

Magnolia stellata belongs to a group of shrubs that needs little or no pruning (see pages 39–41). These are mainly shrubs that do not produce a lot of new replacement growth, and the group includes *Acer* spp. (maple) and *Syringa* spp. (lilac). Any growth tends to be at the end of the branches and stems, and a lot of the plant's energy is directed into producing leaves and flowers. With plants in this group it is important to pay attention to the initial training, so that they have a good, open framework of branches to make up the typical shape of the shrub; remove any crossing or rubbing branches at the early, formative stages.

Early-flowering shrubs

The following shrubs bear flowers on old wood and, so that they have time to produce plenty of strong, new shoots on which flowers will be borne the following spring, they should be cut back after flowering:

- *Buddleja alternifolia*
- *Chaenomeles* spp. (flowering quince)
- *Cytisus* spp. and cultivars (broom) except *C.* 'Porlock'
- *Deutzia* spp.
- *Exochorda* spp.
- *Forsythia* spp.
- *Kerria japonica*
- *Philadelphus* spp.
- *Prunus glandulosa; P. triloba* (flowering almond)
- *Ribes* spp. (flowering currant) – deciduous forms only
- *Rubus* spp. – flowering forms only
- *Spiraea* 'Arguta'
- *Stephanandra* spp.
- *Weigela* cultivars

Pruning a weigela

Prune shrubs such as weigelas, which bear flowers on shoots produced during the previous year, as soon as the flowers have faded.

Once the shrub is mature, the main pruning is to remove any dead, dying or diseased wood. Weak shoots or untypical shoots should also be removed. This is usually done after flowering, although dead and damaged branches can also be removed in late summer.

My forsythia has become overgrown and hardly produces any flowers. Can I do something about this?

Yes, you can. When the pruning of forsythia is neglected, the shrub becomes choked with old wood, which reduces the number of flowering shoots that can be produced. If it still produces flowers, wait until they have faded and then cut away all the straggly and misplaced shoots. Then take out some of the oldest, thickest branches, cutting them low down, close to ground level. Make sure that you remove branches from the centre of the plant so that light can penetrate to all parts of the shrub. Several other overgrown deciduous shrubs can be treated in the same way, including *Berberis* spp.; *Clethra alnifolia* (sweet pepper bush); *C. arborea* (lily-of-the-valley tree); *Corylopsis* spp. (winter hazel); *Cotoneaster* spp.; *Cytisus battandieri; Hydrangea macrophylla* and cultivars; *Kolkwitzia amabilis* (beauty bush); *Potentilla fruticosa* and cultivars (shrubby cinquefoil); *Ribes sanguineum* (flowering currant); and *Symphoricarpos* spp. (snowberry).

***Forsythia* × *intermedia* 'Lynwood'**

Summer-flowering deciduous shrubs

When is the best time to prune shrubs that flower in late summer?

It is best to prune shrubs in this group in the late spring of the following year. If they are pruned immediately after the flowers have faded, the young shoots that develop will be damaged by winter frosts. If you put off pruning until the following year, the fresh young shoots should not be exposed to frosts.

First, cut out dead and diseased shoots, and then remove all those that cross the centre of the shrub. At the same time, cut out any thin or weak shoots. To encourage the production of flowering shoots, cut all those shoots that produced flowers in the previous summer to just above a bud.

Someone told me to cut my buddleia to the ground each year. Should I do this?

***Buddleja davidii* 'Mongo'**

If it is *Buddleja davidii* the answer is yes, but many other buddleias do not need such drastic treatment. *B. davidii* is one of a group of plants that flower on new wood, and to prevent the shrub getting too large and lanky it is normally cut back almost to ground level, to the first strong bud above the previous year's pruning. This should be done in early spring, just as growth is beginning, so that by flowering time strong, new growth will have developed. Over the years it is possible that the base will become a little overcrowded, but this congestion can be relieved by removing one or two of the older stubs. Any that die back to the base should also be removed.

Pruning late-flowering deciduous shrubs

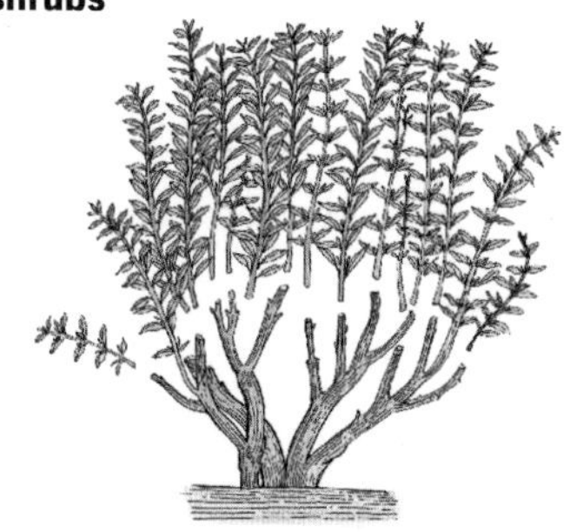

Buddleja davidii should be pruned in early spring, when flowered shoots are removed to within a few buds of the old wood.

Shrubs to cut back hard

The following deciduous shrubs, which produce flowers on new wood, can be cut back in spring, just before the plant begins to show signs of growth:

- *Buddleja davidii; B.* 'Lochinch'
- *Caryopteris* × *clandonensis*
- *Ceanothus* spp. – deciduous forms only
- *Ceratostigma plumbaginoides; C. willmottianum*
- *Clerodendrum bungei*
- *Fuchsia*
- *Hydrangea paniculata*
- *Leycesteria formosa*
- *Perovskia*
- *Romneya*

I have several hydrangeas in my garden. How should I prune them?

Hydrangea macrophylla

Most hydrangeas need little pruning, and, unusually, they should not be deadheaded as soon as the flowers go over. Unlike most shrubs that flower on old wood, forms of *Hydrangea macrophylla*, the common mophead and lacecap hydrangeas, should not be pruned immediately after flowering. Instead, plants can be pruned and deadheaded in mid-spring. The dead flower-heads protect the developing young shoots from winter weather; in spring, they are cut off just above a pair of strong buds. Little pruning is needed, apart from the removal of the usual dead, dying or diseased wood, but if old plants are still overcrowded, a few of the older, woodier stems can also be pruned out to allow the development of fresh shoots. This need not be done every year, but the plant will be more vigorous if a few stems are removed every spring.

Exceptions to the general rules are *H. paniculata* and its cultivars, which flower on the current season's wood. In early spring, these should be cut almost to the ground to encourage shoots to develop from the base or to a higher framework of branches.

Pruning hydrangeas

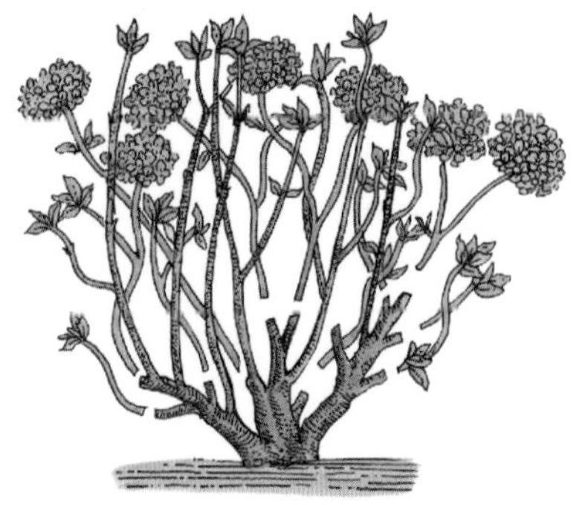

Mophead and lacecap forms of *Hydrangea macrophylla* should be deadheaded and lightly pruned in mid-spring, the old flowerheads being left in place throughout winter to protect the developing young shoots.

How do I prune small, shrubby rock roses?

Cultivars of *Helianthemum* have lots of thin, wiry stems, which would be difficult and time-consuming to prune individually. Usually, they are simply sheared over after flowering, cutting back all the flowering stems to within a short distance of the previous year's wood. Alternatively, they can be lightly trimmed in early spring. The same treatment may also be given to the other rock rose, *Cistus*.

Pruning for foliage and winter colour

I have heard that you can cut some shrubs back drastically to improve their foliage. Is this so?
A number of shrubs, including forms of *Sambucus* (elder) with decorative leaves and *Cotinus* (smoke bush), will produce much larger and more colourful foliage if pruned hard back each spring. If the bush is left, it will produce normal foliage, which will not be as attractive. One drawback to such drastic pruning is that the shrubs are unlikely to flower, so you have to weigh up whether you want foliage or flowers. The pruning method is the same as for *Buddleja davidii* (see page 43).

I would like to introduce some colour into my garden in winter and have heard that some willows are suitable. How should I grow them?

Cornus alba **'Sibirica' (red twig dogwood)**

There are several shrubs that produce attractive bark when the shoots are young but that become quite ordinary as they mature. There are several forms of *Salix* (willow) that can be cut hard back to ground level and that will produce vividly coloured young shoots; if this is done in late winter in alternate years the plants will also bear catkins on the one-year-old stems. *S. acutifolia* 'Blue Streak', for example, produces dark purplish shoots, *S. daphnoides* 'Aglaia' has glossy, brownish-red shoots, and *S.* × *rubens* 'Basfordiana' has yellow stems.

The young shoots of the dogwood *Cornus alba* 'Sibirica' have bright red bark, which shows up well in winter when the foliage has fallen. Left unpruned, this becomes much duller and nowhere near as attractive. In spring, as with willow, cut all the stems back to a good bud at the base. It will quickly grow again and by summer the gap created will again be filled. Some of the brambles with good winter bark, such as *Rubus cockburnianus*, can be treated in the same way. Most of these shrubs have relatively insignificant flowers, but if you wish them to flower then you will have to allow the stems to mature and lose some of the winter colour.

Pruning for winter colour

Use loppers or strong secateurs to cut stems of forms of *Cornus* (dogwood) to about 8cm (3in) above ground level.

***Ceanothus arboreus* 'Trewithen Blue'**

Wall shrubs

How should I prune a ceanothus grown as a wall shrub?

Ceanothus are usually grown as free-standing shrubs, but in cooler climates they are best grown against a protecting wall. When free-grown the evergreens need no pruning, but when they are next to a wall some form of restraint is necessary. Never cut back into the old wood or main stems, but soon after flowering, remove some of the previous season's growth on which the flowers have appeared, back to within a bud or two of old wood. At the same time, either tie in or remove completely any shoots that are sticking out from the wall unless you want a bushy growth. From time to time, cut out one or two of the older stems completely, tying in a new one as a replacement.

I would like to train a *Magnolia grandiflora* against the side of my house. What should I use to support it?

Any shrub grown against a wall will need a support against which it can be trained and to which stems can be tied. Use horizontal wires, held in vine-eyes about 60cm (2ft) apart. Alternatively, erect a trellis, held on battens so that it is 3–5cm (1–2in) away from the wall to allow air to circulate behind the plant.

Remember that plants growing against a wall will be in the rain-shadow cast by the wall. Plant a wall shrub about 45cm (18in) from the wall and train it towards its support with canes or wire. In addition, make sure that you water it regularly.

I have trained a winter-flowering jasmine against a wall. When should I prune it?

The pretty yellow flowers of *Jasminum nudiflorum* appear on the bare stems of this deciduous shrub in winter and early spring. After flowering, the flowered shoots should be cut back to about 8cm (3in) from the ground. Also, fasten in new shoots to the support and shorten sideshoots to three or four buds. This plant is treated differently from the strongly growing climber *Jasminum officinale* (common jasmine), which bears fragrant white flowers from summer to early autumn. These plants should be thinned after flowering, if necessary. At the same time, remove dead and diseased wood and tie in new shoots to their support.

Wall shrubs

Many shrubs can be grown against a wall, and this is a useful way of growing plants that might be too tender for the open garden or ones for which there might not otherwise be space. Among the most popular and reliable are:

- *Abelia floribunda*
- *Berberis* × *stenophylla*
- *Carpenteria californica*
- *Caryopteris* × *clandonensis*
- *Ceanothus* spp.
- *Chaenomeles* × *superba*
- *Clerodendrum trichotomum*
- *Escallonia* cultivars
- *Fremontodendron* cultivars (flannel bush)
- *Magnolia grandiflora*
- *Pyracantha* cultivars

Escallonia **'Donard Seedling'**

Jasminum nudiflorum

I would like to train a wall shrub up the side of my house, but I am worried that this will compromise the security of my home. Is there anything I can do to avoid this?

Most wall shrubs and climbers are too weak or precarious to support an intruder, who would be at risk of injuring or killing himself if attempting to climb them. A well-established wisteria that is securely fixed to the wall, however, might offer an opportunity. To prevent trouble, train it so that no strong stems are near windows, only the weaker growths. If you are worried, then plant a prickly shrub such as pyracanthus or berberis at the base of the wisteria, or grow a strong, climbing rose up through it. The vicious thorns of all these plants should deter anyone climbing the wisteria. Ladders present more of a threat to security than climbers, so ensure they are locked away after being used for pruning.

Hedges and Topiary

Basic techniques

Is hedge-trimming a form of pruning? Most trees and shrubs are pruned to enhance their health and vigour; because they are usually preferred in their natural form they are shaped to a limited extent only. However, some shrubs can be pruned regularly so that they keep a particular desired shape, and the most common use of this feature is when shrubs are used as hedging. To make a hedge, shrubs are grown in a row and trimmed to create a neat and tidy line. Not all hedges are trimmed tightly, and in some settings it is appropriate to allow

Taxus baccata **(yew)**

What is the best way to trim a hedge? The usual way to trim a hedge is with hand shears or with a mechanical hedge-cutter, which may be either petrol-driven or electrically powered. To get a perfectly regular hedge, it is important to use guides of some kind. String or wood straightedges are often used, but it makes life easier if you have a wooden framework which you can place over the hedge each time you cut it. One frame at each end of the hedge – or at regular intervals if it is a long hedge – can be connected by taut string. These frames will enable you to cut the hedge to the same size each time. When hedges are cut free-hand they often get thicker with each cut until one day you suddenly realize that it is twice as wide as it used to be. Keep the blades of the shears or cutters parallel to the hedge and try to avoid dipping the tip into the hedge and making a dent.

Shaping a hedge

Making a template from hardboard or even cardboard is an ideal way of establishing a uniform height and width for a hedge.

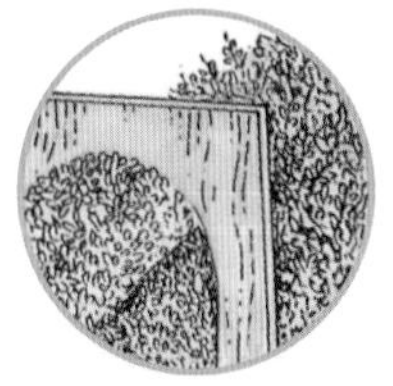

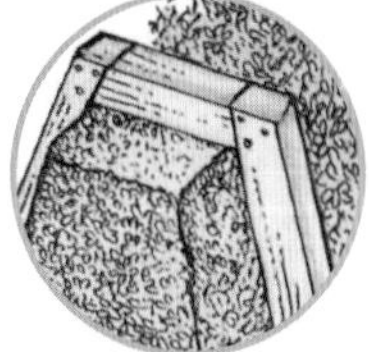

Species	When to prune
Buxus spp. (box)	Late spring and late summer
Carpinus betulus (hornbeam)	Mid- to late summer
Chamaecyparis lawsoniana (lawson cypress)	Late spring and late summer
× *Cupressocyparis leylandii* (leyland cypress)	Late spring, midsummer and early autumn
Crataegus spp. (hawthorn, quickthorn)	Early summer and early autumn
Fagus sylvatica (beech)	Mid- to late summer
Ilex spp. (holly)	Late summer
Lavandula spp. (lavender)	Spring and early autumn
Ligustrum spp. (privet)	Late spring, midsummer and early autumn
Lonicera nitida (poor man's box)	Late spring, midsummer and early autumn
Prunus laurocerasus (cherry laurel)	Mid-spring and late summer
Prunus lusitanicus (Portugal laurel)	Mid-spring and late summer
Taxus spp. (yew)	Mid- to late summer
Thuja plicata (western red cedar)	Mid- to late spring and early autumn

them to grow informally so that they more resemble a line of normal shrubs.

The other main use for tight pruning of this type is to cut shrubs into a variety of shapes, know as topiary (see pages 58–9). Often a few artificial aids are required to create the shape, especially if it is a complicated one, but in general the trimming techniques are similar to those used to create a hedge. Sometimes the two techniques are combined and a hedge, instead of simply being straight lines, has a more 'carved' feel about it with crenellated, undulating or billowing shapes and possibly animals or other shapes included in it.

How often do I need to trim a hedge?

Timing and frequency will vary according to the type of shrub used. *Taxus* spp. (yew), for example, needs cutting once a year, but other, faster-growing shrubs may need to be cut every four to six weeks. The best times to cut for the most common hedging plants are summarized in the table above.

Fagus **(beech)**

***Berberis thunbergii* 'Rose glow' (Japanese barberry)**

Formal and informal hedges

What shape should a hedge be?

Hedges are normally cut so that they are narrower at the top than they are at the bottom. The top is usually flat, although they may be pointed or rounded, either for decorative effect or, in areas with high snowfall, to prevent the snow from piling up on the top and splitting open the hedge (see pages 148–9). The slightly sloping sides and top are usually cut in a neat flat line, but some hedges are deliberately allowed to develop bumps and curves, although this always looks more appropriate with large hedges. Irregular hedges, where the growth rate varies as a result of a mixture of different shrubs, are best suited to growing in a rural setting.

Some hedges never seem to be clipped. Is this bad practice?

This largely depends on the gardener's reasons for not clipping. If the hedge ought to be cut, but for some reason the gardener never gets round to it, it is bad practice because the hedge will eventually become overgrown and it will be a major job to restore it.

Many gardeners, however, grow what are known as informal hedges. These are hedges of a less conventional plant material, such as roses, escallonia or berberis, which are planted in a conventional hedge line but are allowed to grow as normal shrubs with arching stems. This not only gives a more informal appearance to the hedge but also allows flowering wood to be retained so that the hedge produces flowers. The shrubs are pruned in the appropriate way for that particular shrub.

The hedge in my new garden has not been cut for years. Can it be restored?
This will depend on what the shrubs are. If the hedge consists of a conifer such as × *Cupressocyparis leylandii* (leyland cypress) there is little chance, because it will not regenerate from old wood. However, some shrubs will regrow if they are cut hard back, and they are best tackled in several stages (see pages 56–7).

Crataegus spp. (hawthorn) and *Aucuba japonica* (spotted laurel) can be treated even more severely and cut back to the ground. This may seem drastic but it is often a more attractive option than keeping the overgrown hedge for a number of years as you cut first one side, then the other and finally the top.

When the hedge has been cut, keep it watered and fed to help it recover. Once all sides have been cut back and the hedge is recovering, do not forget to clip it in the normal way so as to prevent it from getting out of control again.

Overgrown hedges
The following shrubs can be cut back hard if they have been allowed to become overgrown:
- *Aucuba japonica* (spotted laurel)
- *Carpinus betulus* (hornbeam)
- *Crataegus* spp. (hawthorn)
- *Ilex* spp. (holly)
- *Ligustrum ovalifolium* (privet)
- *Lonicera nitida*
- *Prunus laurocerasus* (cherry laurel)
- *Taxus* spp. (yew)

Informal hedging shrubs
Informal hedges can be created from the following shrubs, which will need minimum cutting back unless they far outgrow their allotted space. Such hedges do take up more room than neatly clipped, formal hedges, so they are not appropriate for small gardens.
- *Berberis* spp.
- *Corylus* spp. (hazel)
- *Cotoneaster* spp.
- *Elaeagnus pungens*
- *Escallonia* cultivars
- *Hebe* spp. (shrubby veronica)
- *Hypericum* spp. (St John's wort)
- *Lavandula* spp. (lavender)
- *Potentilla* spp.
- *Pyracantha* spp.
- *Rhododendron* spp.
- *Salix* spp. (willow)
- *Spiraea* 'Arguta'
- *Tamarix ramosissima* (tamarisk)

Pyracantha rogersiana

Evergreen shrubs

I have a laurel hedge and the hedge-trimmers always leave dead, brown leaves on it. What should I do?

***Prunus laurocerasus* (laurel)**

If you cut a hedge composed of large-leaved shrubs with shears or hedge-trimmers, you are likely to cut a lot of the leaves in half. These either die completely or die back partially, leaving a brown line on the cut margin. It is difficult to avoid this with these tools, and the only way to do it without cutting the leaves in half is with secateurs. Always cut shoots back to just above a leaf joint; new shoots will develop and hide the cuts. Do not position the cuts so that a short piece of stem is left, which will not only be unsightly but may also cause the onset of decay. This makes it a long job, but it certainly makes a better one.

The leaves of *Fagus* spp. (beech) and *Carpinus* spp. (hornbeam) can also be affected in this way, but it takes a patient gardener with plenty of time to tackle a large hedge of these with secateurs, and most will tend to put up with a little browning. It depends on how much of a perfectionist you are.

What is the best way to prune a privet hedge?

Small-leaved evergreen hedges, created from shrubs such as *Ligustrum ovalifolium* (privet) and *Lonicera nitida* (shrubby honeysuckle) and its golden-leaved cultivar 'Baggesen's Gold', are traditionally pruned with hand shears. Modern shears are lighter to use than the old-fashioned models, and they do not judder wrists and hands so violently. Even so, they can still be difficult to use, especially if the hedge is a long one. You might, therefore, prefer to use electrically powered trimmers or even petrol-driven ones. Some types cut on both sides of the blade and some on one only. Do not forget to wear ear muffs and goggles if you use powered trimmers.

***Ligustrum ovalifolium* (privet)**

Large-leaved hedging plants

To prevent unattractive browning and possible die-back, clip back these large-leaved plants used for hedges with secateurs rather than a trimmer:

- *Aucuba japonica* (spotted laurel)
- *Carpinus betulus* (common hornbeam)
- *Fagus sylvatica* (beech)
- *Prunus laurocerasus* (cherry laurel); *P. lusitanica* (Portugal laurel)

Pruning large-leaved evergreens

Large-leaved evergreen shrubs should be pruned with secateurs rather than hedge-trimmers to avoid leaving cut leaves, which will turn brown.

Is it possible to have a flowering evergreen hedge?

Yes, there are several evergreen shrubs that can be used as hedging. Evergreen species of berberis, such as *Berberis darwinii*, which has golden-yellow flowers, and *B. gagnepainii* var. *lanceifolia*, which has bright yellow flowers, both in mid-spring, make dense hedges, which should be pruned once a year after flowering. There are also several cultivars of escallonia that will make dense, neat hedges. *Escallonia* 'Red Elf' has bright red flowers and *E*. 'Donard Seedling' has pink flowers. Escallonias bloom in early summer and then, if left unpruned, on and off until autumn. Once hedges are established, keep them neat by cutting them back after the first flush of flowers has faded.

Rosemary and lavender

Rosmarinus officinalis (rosemary) and *Lavandula* spp. (lavender) make attractive hedges, especially suitable for herb gardens and parterres, but they often become rather straggly, especially if they are not trimmed every year. New growth will not develop when the pruning cuts have been made into the old wood. Rather than cutting them back severely to regenerate them, they are best replaced with young plants. Replace some of the soil if the new hedge is in the same place. Prune the new, young plants in mid-spring to encourage them to adopt a neat, low habit.

Pruning small-leaved hedges

Small-leaved evergreen hedges, such as privet, are often pruned with hand shears.

Longer and larger hedges are often more efficiently cut with a powered hedge-trimmer.

Taxus baccata (yew)

Coniferous hedges

Are coniferous hedges treated in the same way as deciduous shrubs?

Evergreen coniferous hedges, such as *Thuja plicata* (western red cedar), × *Cupressocyparis leylandii* (leyland cypress) and *Chamaecyparis lawsoniana* (lawson cypress) make good, dense hedges, although leyland cypress is too large and vigorous for all but the largest gardens. The main thing to do is to prune the leading shoots when they reach 15–30cm (6–12in) above the desired final height. You should then cut off the tops about 15cm (6in) below this height. This will allow sufficient space for the hedge to create a bushy top, disguising the top of the leader.

I have a yew hedge that has gradually got far too wide and high. How do I reduce it in size?

Renovating an overgrown hedge is possible, but it can take time to do it properly, although the results are worth it. Not all hedge shrubs will respond to severe cutting back, but *Taxus* (yew) and a number of others will survive and benefit from such treatment. The secret is to spread the work over at least three years and sometimes more.

In the first year, cut one side of the hedge severely back, as tight as you wish, to the main stems. It will look dreadful for the remainder of that year and into the next, but it will eventually recover, and from this point it should be trimmed as usual. Cut the top and the other side as usual. If the hedge is recovering well, cut back the top in the same severe way in the following year. If the first side has not put on much growth, leave the top cut for another year. A year later, do the same to the other side of the hedge, again cutting it back tight. Water and feed the hedge so that it has the best chance of recovering.

Other conifers should not be cut back like this, because they will not recover. However, the tops of most conifers can be cut out from young hedges when the desired height has been achieved.

I would like a dense, thick coniferous hedge. Is there an alternative to leylandii or leyland cypress?

***Thuja plicata* 'Can-can' (western red cedar)**

By far the best conifer hedge to grow is one of yew (*Taxus baccata*), even though strictly speaking it is not a conifer as it does not have cones. It is perceived as slow growing, which it is in comparison to the fast-growing leyland cypress (× *Cupressocyparis leylandii*), but you will still have a reasonable hedge within five years and a good one in eight. The beauty of yew, in addition to its appearance, is that it only requires cutting once a year, and unlike most other conifers, if it does get out of control, it can be heavily pruned to bring it back to size and retain the shape. Most other conifers will not regenerate, and are likely to die if old wood is pruned.

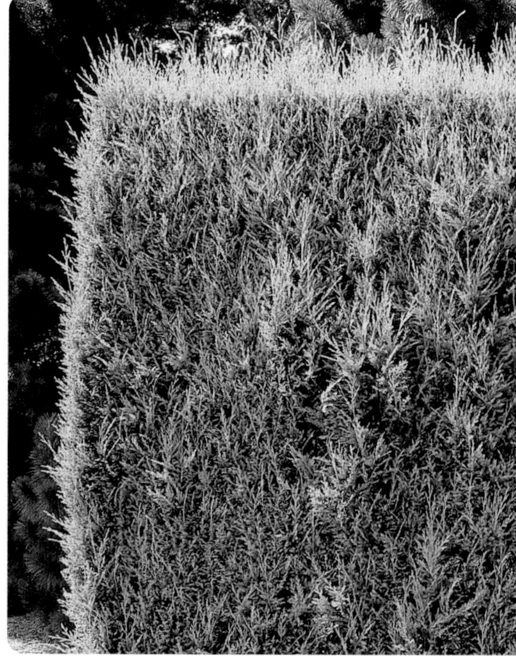

× *Cupressocyparis leylandii* (leyland cypress)

Leylandii and its various forms make good hedges, but they will only do so if they receive plenty of attention: even one season's neglect will see problems start. It is impossible to cut back into old wood without creating an area without foliage in the hedge; more often the tree dies, creating a gap in the hedge. Leylandii's relation, macrocarpa (*Cupressus macrocarpa*) has similar faults.

The thujas, *Thuja plicata* and *T. occidentalis* in particular, present a better bet. These have the dense shagginess of the leylandii, but are slower-growing and respond well to being pruned only twice a year, in late spring and again in late summer.

***Carpinus betulus* (hornbeam)**

Deciduous hedges

Which plants are best for a formal deciduous hedge?

The best plants for such a hedge are *Fagus sylvatica* (beech), *Carpinus betulus* (hornbeam) and *Crataegus monogyna* (hawthorn). Beech forms a fairly high, thick hedge, with superbly coloured leaves in autumn. Even when the colours fade, the leaves remain on the hedge for several months. The eventual size of beech hedges – they can get to 3m (10ft) or more high – often deters gardeners from planting them. Newly planted beech hedges must be cut back by one-third to a half immediately to encourage the development of shoots from each plant's base. Once established, use hand shears or powered trimmers to trim it to shape in mid- or late summer.

Clip hedges of hornbeam to shape with hand shears in midsummer, and hawthorn can be pruned to shape any time after the flowers have faded until late winter. Neglected hawthorn hedges can be cut back hard in late summer.

How do I go about creating a deciduous hedge?

As with any new garden project, the ground must be prepared thoroughly before planting. Dig it deeply and add plenty of well-rotted organic material. The planting distances vary according to hedging material, but the young shrubs are usually placed between 30 and 60cm (1–2ft) apart. If you are planting bare-root shrubs, plant between late autumn and early spring; container-grown plants can be planted at any time, as long as the ground is not frozen or waterlogged. Once the shrubs have been planted, the main and any strong sideshoots are cut back by between a half and one-third of their original length.

In the following year, between late autumn and early spring, this process is repeated.

Although it may seem rather drastic, and to be losing too much of the plant, the severe pruning prevents the base of the hedge from becoming unsightly and bare. In the third and subsequent winters, cut back all new shoots by about one-third. The growth that develops in the following spring and summer will be bushy and start to form a thick, solid screen of leaves. Remember to water the hedge regularly until it is established and to feed it in spring and early summer to encourage it to produce young shoots.

Some deciduous shrubs, such as *Crataegus* spp. (hawthorn, quickthorn), are fast-growing and should be cut back hard, to at least half their length. Any laterals that grow beyond the desired width of the hedge should be cut back to within it, so that a thick framework develops. Once the hedge of either type reaches the desired height and width, it is trimmed back as a normal mature hedge.

Crataegus oxyacantha **'Paul's Scarlet' (hawthorn)**

Establishing a formal hedge

1 Immediately after planting, cut back the leader and sideshoots by between a half and one-third.

2 Repeat the process in the following winter.

3 In the third winter, cut back all new shoots by about one-third.

Topiary

How often do I need to trim topiary?
Although this will depend on the shrub that is used, topiary will need to be clipped at least once a year and probably more often. *Taxus* (yew) is fairly slow-growing, but it will need more than one trim a year if you want to keep it looking really crisp. *Buxus* (box) will also keep a neat, tight shape with minimal pruning, but other looser shrubs, with larger leaves, such as privet, will need more frequent trims.

Although it is a climber, I believe that ivy can be used for topiary. How can I achieve this?
Yes, many of the small-leaved forms of *Hedera* (ivy) can be used for topiary when they are successfully grown over a wire former. The plant should be clipped back tight to keep it in shape. It is fairly easy to make a former for a pyramid or cone from wire for yourself, but for more ambitious designs it is possible to buy some fairly intricate shapes from garden centres. Ivy plants are relatively quick-growing, and it is important to prune it regularly to make sure that no stray stems spoil the shape.

***Buxus* (box) topiary cockerel**

Box clipped into topiary balls

Plants for topiary
Plants used for topiary should ideally have small leaves, a dense habit and fairly pliable stems. The following are suitable subjects for training in a range of shapes:
- *Buxus sempervirens* (box)
- *Hedera* spp. (ivy)
- *Ilex* spp. (holly)
- *Laurus nobilis* (bay)
- *Ligustrum ovalifolium* (oval-leaved privet)
- *Lonicera nitida* (box-leaved honeysuckle); *L. nitida* 'Baggesen's Gold'
- *Taxus baccata* (yew)
- *Thuja occidentalis* (arborvitae)

How do I prune a shrub to get a topiary shape?

Geometric shapes are not too difficult to cut from existing shrubs, but one of the problems of trying to make a more complex shape from an established shrub is that within the plant is an intricate network of branches. In order to get your shape, you may have to cut through some of these, which immediately removes part of the bush, possibly leaving a hole.

It is better and easier to start from scratch with a young plant, or at least to begin training a shrub that is much smaller than the ultimate size of the topiary so that you can train the individual shoots as they develop. For complex shapes, it may be necessary to construct a wire former, but in many cases the shape can be achieved by tying the shoots in position with a piece of tarred string. It is easier to use new shoots for training because older ones are often rigid and will not bend, and may even break if pushed too hard. Young, more pliant, shoots are more readily bent into position. Allow the appropriate shoots to develop and tie these to the former or into other shoots, removing any others that are not needed. Allow sideshoots to develop and fill out the shape and trim off anything that grows outside the shape. Gradually the plant will fill out and the topiary will take on a definite form.

Taxus spp. (yew) are the only shrubs that have stems that are flexible enough to bend and train into complex shapes, and yew is always the first choice for figurative work. Keeping flat shapes flat is surprisingly difficult, and the use of a wooden former or string guidelines is usually essential. Round shapes are easier to cut by eye, but it always helps if there is a former to which the shrub was originally trained left inside the plant, which can be used as a guide for trimming.

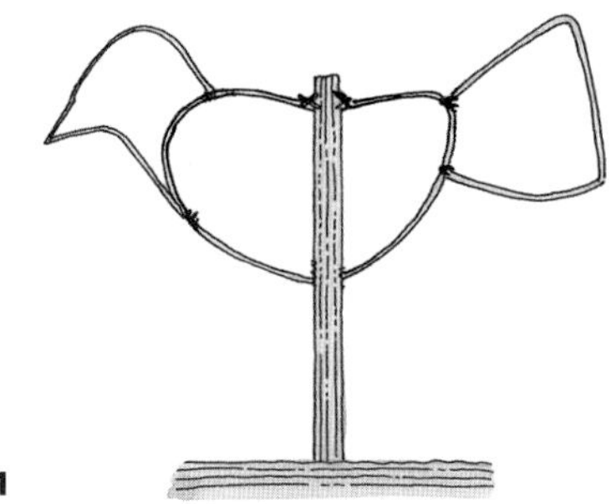

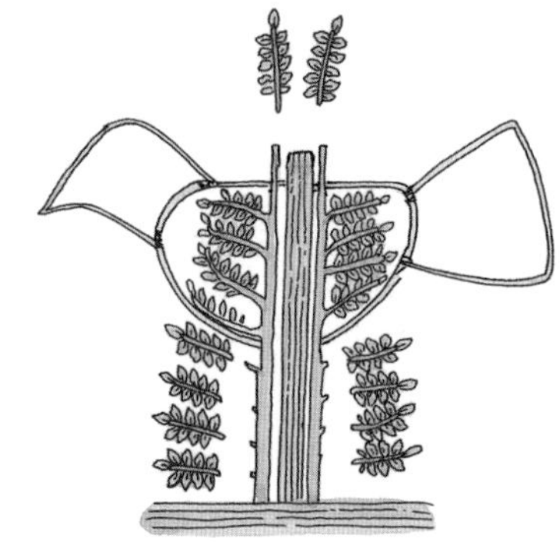

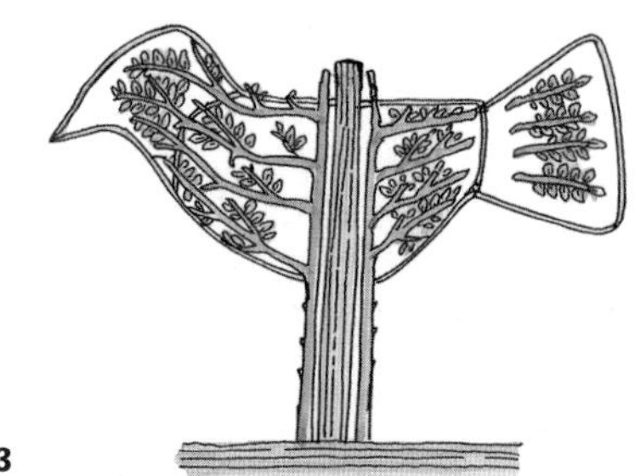

1 Choose a simple shape and use a wire former to which the shoots can be tied.

2 Plant two young shrubs near the former. Loosely tie them in and cut any shoots outside the former.

3 As shoots develop, keep cutting them back to encourage the development of dense growth inside the former.

Climbers

Basic techniques

What are climbing plants and do they need pruning?

A climbing plant is one that needs support from another plant, walls, fences or structures such as arches, pergolas, arbours, poles or peasticks. If it is not supported, it simply flops on the ground. Some climbers – *Hedera* spp. (ivy), for example – cling to their support. Others, such as clematis, have tendrils, which bind them to the support, and still others, including *Lonicera* spp. (honeysuckle) and *Humulus lupulus* (hop), twist their way around the support. Many are perennial but some, such as *Lathyrus odoratus* (sweet pea), are annuals.

Some climbers need no or little pruning, but the majority benefit from regular attention. As with all shrubby plants, they will flower and fruit better and generally look much healthier if they are looked after. Deadheading will often encourage a second flush of flowers. If the plant has attractive fruit or seedheads, such as rose hips, they are worth leaving. It is always important to remove dead, dying, damaged or diseased wood. There are also other practical reasons for pruning. An unpruned climber may eventually become too heavy for its support, which could collapse under the weight, especially in a strong wind. In addition, unpruned and untrained climbers will produce long stems that whip around in the wind, causing damage not only to other plants but possibly also to you or a visitor to your garden.

Types of climber

Climbing plants fall into four main groups:

- Scrambling climbers, such as *Jasminum nudiflorum* and *Bougainvillea* spp., have flexible stems that must be tied into a framework of wires or trellis.
- Twining climbers, including *Wisteria* spp. and *Jasminum officinale*, have stems that twist around a support, such as trellis or wire.
- Self-clinging climbers, including *Hedera* spp. (ivy) and *Hydrangea anomala* subsp. *petiolaris*, are entirely self-supporting.
- Tendril climbers, such as *Vitis coignetiae* and *Passiflora caerulea* (passionflower), cling to their supports with modified leaves or stems.

Passiflora caerulea **(passionflower)**

When should I prune a climber?

As with shrubs and bushes, pruning time depends largely on the production of flowers or fruit. One group consists of those climbers that flower in summer on the current year's growth; late-flowering clematis, for example, are in this category, and they are cut back at some point between late winter and early spring, just before growth begins. All congested, misplaced, dead or damaged wood should be removed first. Also cut out one or two of the main stems from the base to promote fresh growth. All sideshoots should be cut back to five or six buds, from which new shoots will emerge to carry that season's flowers.

The second main group are those that flower in the early part of the year on old wood produced during the previous summer, and these are pruned immediately after flowering. Again, cut out all dead and damaged wood and any weak or congested stems. Remove all the shoots that have flowered to one or a pair of good buds, and this will produce the growth for next year's flowers. Repeat this every year.

How important is early training?

This is an important aspect of growing climbers which should not be overlooked. Left untrained, many climbers would simply climb a wall or other support in a single tangled column. Always try to make sure the plant spreads out as much as possible, and that the shoots form a fan at the base at an early stage to establish a good framework of stems. After planting, most climbers benefit from being cut back to promote the growth of sideshoots. Cut back to an outward-facing bud – that is, one that points along the wall or trellis. To prevent the climber from taking up too much space, it may be necessary to remove altogether any shoots that face away from the wall or support.

As with wall shrubs, climbers are planted a little distance from their support, especially if it is a wall, and this means that the young shoots should be tied to sloping canes to direct the new growth towards the wall or trellis. In the following winter, the shoots, including the leader, can again be cut back to a strong bud, reducing the new wood by about half. This will promote vigorous growth and help create a good framework. As the climber grows, cut out all crossing wood and any stems that are dead or damaged.

***Campsis* spp.**

Are the pruning cuts the same as for shrubs?

Basically, yes. Make clean cuts that slope slightly away from a good bud or pair of buds. It is also important to maintain a good structure and to promote young, vigorous growth. The main difference is that training does not finish after the plant matures as it does with a shrub. You have be vigilant and tie growing shoots, positioning them where they will give the best display as well as obtaining good support and plenty of light.

Clinging and tendril climbers

How do I prune an ivy that is covering a whole wall?

It is almost impossible to get a self-clinging plant like *Hedera* spp. (ivy) or *Parthenocissus* spp. (Virginia creeper) down from a wall once it is established, but fortunately they do not require much pruning. Apart from the regular removal of dead, damaged or diseased wood, which should be done in late winter or early spring, the only pruning that is needed is to keep them under control. Climbers like this can quickly cover windows if they are not kept cut back, and they can even get into gutters and push under roof tiles. It is important to regularly prune back such climbers once or just before they reach roof level.

***Hedera Helix* 'Angularis Aurea' (English ivy)**

Self-supporting climbers

The following climbers will need no extra support beyond initial training towards a wall or trellis. Climbers like *Hedera* spp. (ivy) climb by means of their aerial roots; plants such as *Parthenocissus* spp. produce tendrils that both twine and have adhesive tips; plants such as *Passiflora* spp. have tendrils.

- *Ampelopsis* spp.
- *Campsis* spp. (trumpet creeper, trumpet vine)
- *Hedera canariensis* (Algerian ivy); *H. colchica* (Persian ivy); *H. helix* (common ivy)
- *Hydrangea anomala* subsp. *petiolaris* (climbing hydrangea)
- *Parthenocissus henryana* (Chinese Virginia creeper); *P. quinquefolia* (Virginia creeper); *P. tricuspidata* (Boston ivy)
- *Passiflora caerulea* (passionflower)
- *Schizophragma hydrangeoides*
- *Vitis* 'Brant'; *V. coignetiae*

Is it true that climbers should not be allowed to climb up walls?

A well-maintained wall is likely to be unharmed by ivy, but the aerial roots of ivy end in little 'adhesive' pads, which attach themselves to a support and find their way into the tiniest gaps. For this reason, most people prefer not to allow ivy to grow over a house wall built of porous bricks and mortar.

Are ornamental vines pruned in the same way as fruiting grape vines?

Yes, if space is limited, but this is not the best way to display the decorative foliage of these ornamental forms of *Vitis*. More frequently they are grown for their foliage and the shade that this provides, and this means that they are usually left unpruned to climb over a pergola or arbour. Dead or damaged wood should be pruned out, of course, and if they become too large for the space they can be cut back in winter. They can also be grown against a wall for decorative effect. Here they can also be allowed to grow unpruned, but since space will be at more of a premium they can be pruned like fruit vines (see pages 142–5), although they need not be kept quite so rigidly in check.

How should I tackle an overgrown climber?

This is not always easy, because some climbers will not respond to being cut back hard and the only easy way is to start again. Most climbers that will not recover are old or are not in good condition. However, it can be worth attempting to renovate a neglected climber, which has developed a tangle of old, congested wood and that is producing a few flowers high up. Pruning to renovate is best done in spring.

Cut back as much of the old wood as you can, beginning with the twiggy shoots and then cutting back all the stems to about 50cm (20in) from the ground. Water well the day before and after pruning and add some liquid feed to the watering. An old climber can be renovated by taking out a few main stems at a time over a period of three or four years. The main difficulty is in removing the stems you have cut out without breaking the remaining ones. It is usually easier to cut a stem into several sections so that you can remove it bit by bit. As new shoots appear, train them in carefully so that they do not grow through those stems still waiting to be removed.

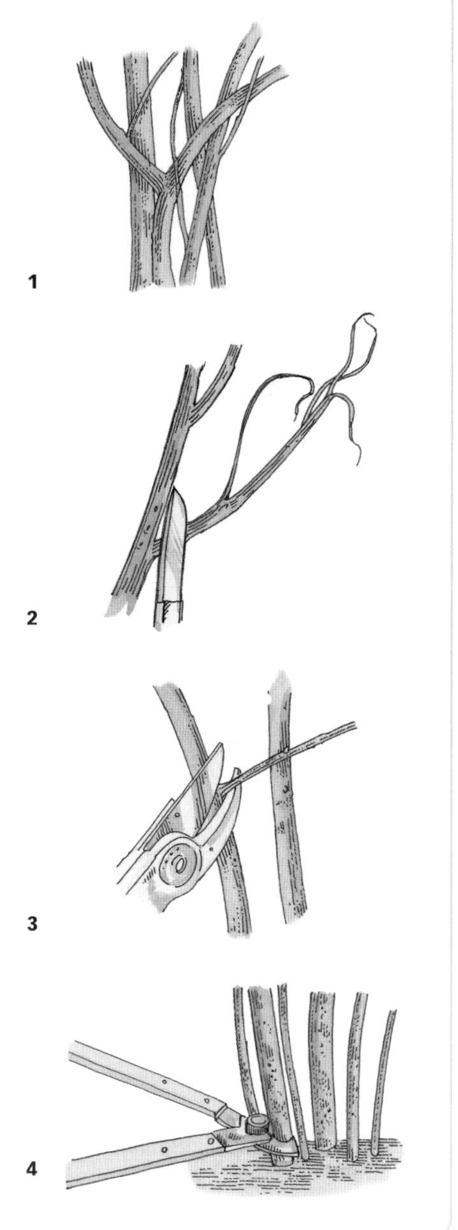

1 Cut out any old, congested growth and shoots that have become entangled.

2 Use sharp secateurs or a knife to completely remove any stems that are damaged or diseased.

3 At the same time, cut back diseased shoots to strong and healthy ones.

4 Climbers that develop new stems from the base can be cut close to ground level; otherwise, cut the main stems back to about 50cm (20in).

***Lonicera periclymenum* 'Belgica' (early Dutch honeysuckle)**

Twining and scrambling climbers

My honeysuckle seems to grow into a tangled mass. How do I prune it?

Some of the most widely grown honeysuckles, including *Lonicera periclymenum* (common honeysuckle, woodbine), *L. periclymenum* 'Belgica' (early Dutch honeysuckle) and *L. periclymenum* 'Serotina' (late Dutch honeysuckle), naturally produce a tangled mass of stems. There is actually nothing wrong with the plant, but it does look a bit of a mess and the flowering tends to get further from the ground and cannot be easily seen. It may be possible to restore the plant simply by cutting out all the dead wood that has accumulated under the new growth, just leaving the live wood. If this still leaves too much of a tangle, cut all the major stems back in spring to about 50cm (20in) from the ground and allow the plant to start again.

I have a Russian vine growing over my garage. How can I control it?

Fallopia baldschuanica is an extremely vigorous, twining climber; it is also a fast-growing plant (also known as the mile-a-minute plant), and the only way to keep it within bounds is to prune it severely each year. It can be cut back to the base in early spring with no loss of flowers.

If you want to grow this plant, it is a best to grow it where it can be left to its own devices, and this means that it is not a suitable choice for a small garden.

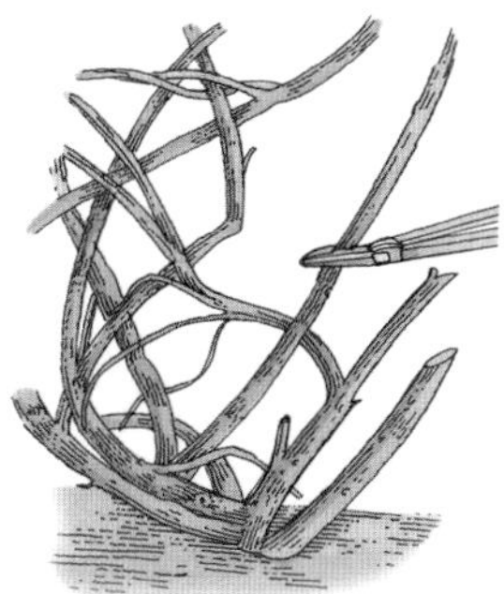

In spring, use loppers or strong secateurs to remove all the old, woody growth.

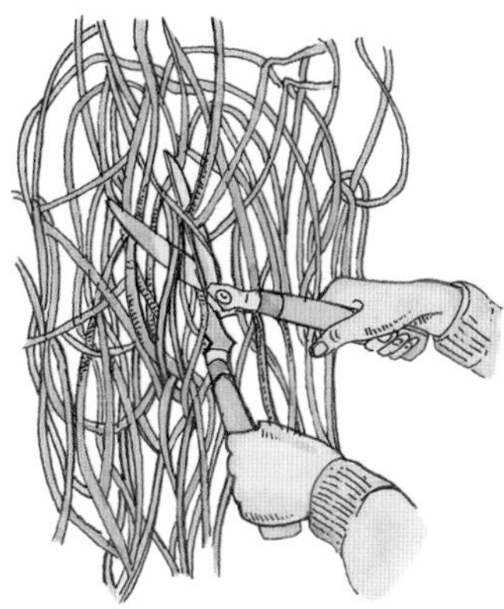

A mass of thin, tangled shoots can be cut back with hand shears.

Do hops need pruning?

No. *Humulus lupulus* (hop) is a hardy perennial, which dies back below ground each autumn and re-emerges in spring. The many stems twine up their supports and need no pruning unless they outstrip their allotted space. They will grow straight up in a tangled mass if left unattended, but it is easy to train the emerging stems so that they are spread out at the base, making them cover a large area. Hops have rough stems and leaves and can leave nasty weals or burns on the skin, so cover up well when you are handling them.

Humulus lupulus **'Aureus' (hops)**

Clematis: Group 1

I have heard that pruning clematis is complicated. Is this true?

Pruning clematis can be confusing, especially if you do not know the name of the particular plant, because there are three different methods of pruning clematis. However, once you know which group your plants belong in and therefore the type of pruning required it will soon become routine. Group 1 contains early-flowering species and hybrids that bear flowers from late spring to midsummer on shoots produced in the previous year. This means that in any one year, as well as flowering on the previous year's growth, the plant is also producing shoots that will bear flowers later in the same year, creating a second and welcome flush of colour in late summer and sometimes into early autumn.

Group 2 is formed of vigorous spring- and early summer-flowering plants that bear flowers on short shoots that arise from growths that developed in the previous year and on the tips of the current season's growth.

Group 3 includes the late-flowering, large-flowered cultivars, some small-flowered cultivars and late-flowering species. These clematis bear flowers in summer and autumn on shoots produced in the same season. Clematis in this group begin new growth in spring each year by developing fresh, young shoots from the ends of old shoots. If these plants are left unpruned, therefore, bases of plants soon become bare and unsightly.

Even if you do not know the name of the clematis in your garden, you can usually work it out by noticing when your plants flower.

I have an old *Clematis montana* that is terribly overgrown. Is there anything I can do about it?

This often happens with montana clematis, which are vigorous plants and can become congested in a small space. If you have room, allow the clematis to climb up into a tall tree, when you need do nothing more. In a more

C. montana 'Tetrarose'

Group 1 clematis

The following evergreen and early-flowering clematis are pruned after flowering. Cut out dead and damaged stems and shorten any others that seem to be outgrowing their space. The aim is to encourage the production of healthy, well-placed new shoots during the year on which next season's flowers will be borne.

- *C. alpina* and cultivars, including 'Constance', 'Frances Rivis', 'Jaqueline du Pré' and 'Pamela Jackman'
- *C. armandii* and cultivars, including 'Apple Blossom'
- *C.* × *cartmanii* 'Avalanche', *C.* × *cartmanii* 'Joe'
- *C. cirrhosa*, *C. cirrhosa* var. *balearica* and cultivars, including 'Freckles'
- *C. macropetala*
- *C. montana* and associated hybrids
- *C. paniculata* 'Bodnant'

Pruning Group 1 clematis

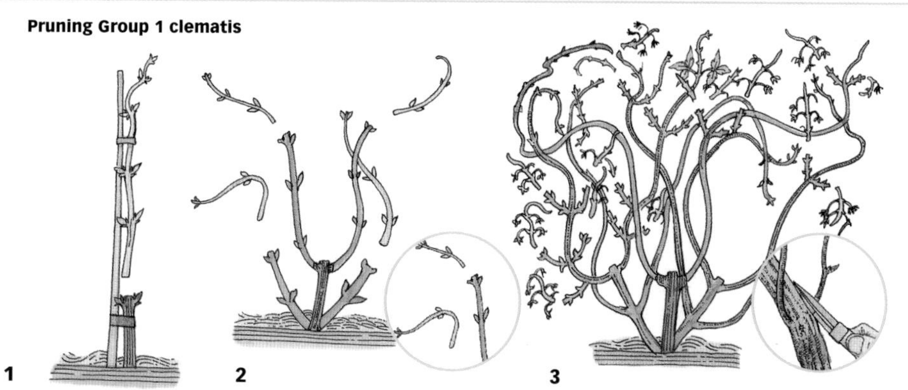

1 In late winter of the first year after being planted, cut the stem to slightly above the lowest pair of healthy buds to encourage the development of strong shoots that will help to form the climber's framework. In summer, space out and secure these stems to a permanent framework of wires or trellis. The initial training of shoots is important to ensure that light and air are able to reach the shoots.

2 In late winter of the second year, cut back by half the lengths of the main shoots that developed in the previous year and were secured to a supporting framework. Make sure that each shoot is cut back to slightly above a pair of healthy buds. If shoots low down on the climber develop flowers early in the year, cut them back to one pair of buds from their base. In summer, fresh shoots will grow; space these out and secure them to the framework.

3 In early summer of the following and subsequent years, use secateurs to cut back all growth that produced flowers earlier in the year to one or two buds from their point of origin. Within this group, *C. montana* and *C. montana* var. *sericea* are vigorous and sometimes left unpruned. This eventually creates a tangled plant. Rejuvenate by cutting to near ground level in late winter.

confined space – on a trellis, for example – it will become so heavy that it may eventually break its support. If the situation is not too severe you can do a lot by removing all the dead wood – there is usually masses of it – and cutting all the previous year's growth back to a single pair of buds. This should be done after flowering.

If it is still too large, cut out some of the older wood, but remember to leave a good selection of shoots with this year's buds on them. From now on, prune reasonably hard each year, cutting back the previous year's growth to just a few buds. If this still leaves too much growth, cut out one or two of the main stems back to the older wood. Tie in any new shoots that develop, training them away from the existing ones if possible, and gradually remove these older stems each year so that eventually the whole climber is renewed. Give the ground around the roots a good soaking the day before you prune and again after you have finished and keep the soil reasonably moist until it has re-established. Liquid feed before and after, added to the water, may also help it recover.

Can you tell me about pruning early-flowering species clematis?

These are, perhaps, the easiest clematis to deal with because they do not need much pruning at all, apart from the removal of dead or diseased material. Some – *C. montana*, for example – can get really large, outgrowing their allocated space. If this is likely, plants can be cut back each year after flowering to within one or two buds of the old wood.

Clemantis: Group 2

I have a lot of large-flowered hybrid clematis in my garden. How are these pruned?

If these are early-flowering clematis, they belong in Group 2, which includes clematis that bear flowers on new sideshoots that are produced on wood formed during the previous year's growing season. These need to be pruned in late winter before the new growth begins. As always, start with dead or damaged wood and proceed to the living stem. Cut back last year's stems until you come to the first pair of strong buds. This should leave most of the framework intact. New shoots will appear from these buds and form the wood on which the flowers will appear.

1 In late winter after planting, cut back the stem to the lowest pair of strong, healthy buds. In late spring and early summer, young shoots should be trained and secured to a framework of wires or a wooden trellis. Shoots will also develop from ground level and these, too, should be trained to the framework. Occasionally, a few flowers are produced in the first year.

2 In late winter of the second year, cut back by half all the main shoots that were produced in the previous year, severing them just above a pair of strong, healthy buds. In the following summer, train the new shoots and space them out on the supporting framework. In this second season, plants usually develop a few flowers on new growth, often into autumn. Creating a strong framework of shoots is essential.

3 In early and midsummer of the third and subsequent years, immediately after the flowers have faded, cut out one-quarter to one-third of mature shoots to within 30cm (12in) of the plant's base. When plants are grown against a wall, the shoots can be readily reached, but when plants are grown on, say, a pergola and stems cannot be untangled plants are best left unpruned.

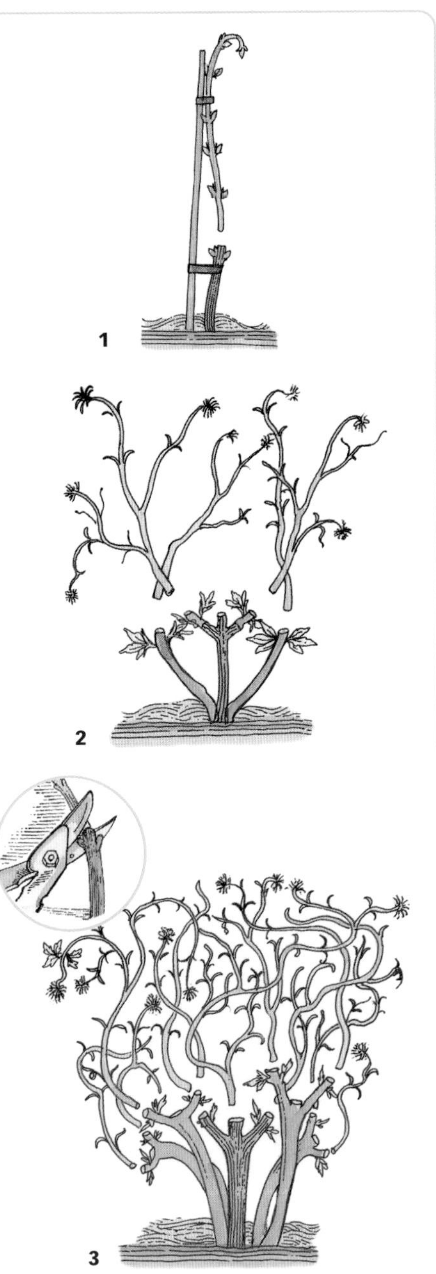

What would happen if I did not bother pruning my clematis at all?

Not a lot at first, but eventually the plants would become bare around the base, and the flowers would be borne further and further up the plant, gradually becoming smaller and fewer. Pruning ensures that the plant produces fresh, healthy growth each year. It also removes potentially diseased wood.

I have a clematis that does not climb. How do I prune it?

Non-climbing clematis include herbaceous plants (which die back at the end of each season) and some sub-shrubs (which produce annual stems that die back to the woody base at the end of the season). These plants are cut back to ground level or to the woody base in late winter. They include: *C.* × *aromatica*; *C.* × *durandii*; *C.* × *eriostemon* and 'Blue Boy' and 'Hendersonii'; *C. heracleifolia*; *C. integrifolia* and 'Alba', 'Pangbourne Pink', 'Rosea' and 'Tapestry'; *C.* × *jouiniana* 'Cote d'Azur'; *C. stans*; and 'Alionushka', 'Arabella' and 'Campanile'.

Large-flowered hybrids

Some clematis catalogues classify these superb hybrids into six groups. To simplify their pruning, however, they can be arranged into two main groups. For example, jackmanii, texensis and viticella types can be pruned in the way suggested for Group 3, while florida, lanuginosa and patens types may be pruned as recommended for Group 2.

Group 2 clematis

The following large-flowered, early- to mid-season flowering clematis bear flowers on sideshoots that develop from stems that grew in the previous year. The aim of pruning is to remove dead and damaged stems before the plant begins to grow in early spring, and to cut back all remaining stems to strong buds, from which new shoots will develop. If plants are deadheaded, a second flush of flowers often appears in late summer.

- *C. florida* and associated hybrids, including 'Belle of Woking', 'Duchess of Edinburgh' and 'Vyvyan Pennell'
- Lanuginosa hybrids, including 'Beauty of Worcester', 'Carnaby', 'Général Sikorski', 'Henryi', 'Marie Boisselot', 'Mrs Cholmondeley', 'Nelly Moser' and 'W.E. Gladstone'
- *C. patens* and associated hybrids, including 'Asao', 'Barbara Dibley', 'Barbara Jackman', 'Bees' Jubilee', 'Countess of Lovelace', 'Daniel Deronda', 'Doctor Ruppel', 'Elsa Späth', 'Gillian Blades', 'H.F. Young', 'Lasurstern', 'Miss Bateman', 'Mrs N. Thompson' and 'The President'
- Other large-flowered hybrids, such as 'Corona' and 'Niobe'

***Clematis* 'Nelly Moser'**

Clematis 'Bill MacKenzie'

Clematis: Group 3

Which clematis flower late in summer and how should I prune them?
Late-flowering clematis include many large-flowered cultivars, which bear flowers in late summer and early autumn on shoots produced during the current year, and some small-flowered cultivars and late-flowering species, which also flower on shoots produced in the current year, but these are borne from summer to late autumn. These clematis should be pruned in early spring, when shoots should be cut back to a pair of strong buds about 20cm (8in) above ground level.

I would like to plant a clematis in my garden that produces large, feathery seedheads. What sort of clematis should I choose and when should I prune it?
Many of the clematis in the orientalis and tangutica groups produce attractive seedheads, and these plants belong in pruning Group 3.

Neglected Group 3 clematis
If a plant in this group is neglected, cut half of the stems back into older wood to encourage the development of shoots from ground level; cut the others back to buds. The following year, cut back the other half.

Clematis 'Rouge Cardinal'

Group 3 clematis
Clematis in this group include the late-flowering, large-flowered cultivars, which have flowers on the current year's growth. Pruning in spring is aimed at producing vigorous shoots on which flowers will be borne later in the same year.

- *C. crispa*
- *C. flammula*
- Jackmanii hybrids, including 'Ascotiensis', 'Comtesse de Bouchaud', 'Ernest Markham', 'Gipsy Queen', 'Hagley Hybrid', 'Lady Betty Balfour', 'Perle d'Azur' and 'Rouge Cardinal'
- *C. orientalis*
- *C. tangutica* and associated hybrids, including 'Bill MacKenzie'
- *C. texensis* and associated hybrids, including 'Duchess of Albany', 'Étoile Rose' and 'Gravetye Beauty'
- *C. viticella* and associated hybrids, including 'Ernest Markham', 'Little Nell', 'Madame Julia Correvon', 'Royal Velours' and 'Star of India'

I love the viticella clematis. How are they pruned?

Viticella clematis belong with other late-flowering cultivars and species in pruning Group 3. These are relatively easy to prune once you have identified what they are. The flowers are produced on the current wood and so all the old wood is redundant and can be cut out. Late in each winter, cut back all the stems to a pair of strong buds 20–30cm (8–12in) from the ground. That is it: there is nothing else to do. Because they are cut almost to the ground they make excellent climbers to grow through other shrubs, especially early-flowering ones. These have usually finished flowering and are looking rather dull by the time the clematis reaches its full height and flowers. When they are grown through shrubs or other climbers, these clematis tend to be self-supporting, but if you are growing them over a trellis you may have to tie in stray shoots from time to time.

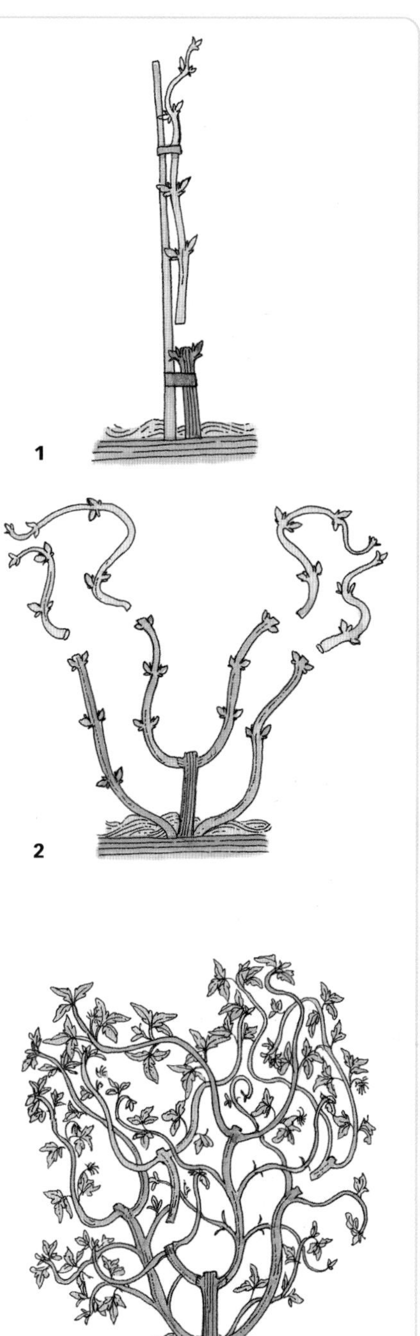

1 In late winter after planting, cut back the main shoot to the lowest pair of strong buds to encourage fresh shoots to develop. In the following summer, the young shoots that develop must be trained and secured against a wire or wooden framework.

2 In late winter of the second year, cut back each shoot to two or three pairs of strong buds. This includes shoots that developed from ground level in the previous year and are starting to form a bushy plant. In the following summer, vigorous shoots develop and, again, they must be spaced out and secured to a supporting framework. From mid- to late summer, flowers will appear on shoots produced earlier in the same season.

3 In late winter of each subsequent year, cut all growths back to leave a pair of strong buds at their base. In the same way as in the previous years, shoots will grow from these buds and bear flowers from midsummer to autumn. Tie shoots to a framework.

Wisteria sinensis (Chinese wisteria)

Wisteria

Is wisteria as difficult to prune as they say?

Pruning wisteria always seems difficult until you have done it a couple of times, and then the routine becomes second nature and you wonder what the fuss was all about. The main deterrent to growing a wisteria is that it needs to be pruned twice a year, and it can be all too easy to forget.

Wisteria is usually grown as an espalier along horizontal, parallel wires fixed to a wall. The initial training is important, and it takes several years to get a good framework of branches. Plant in winter and take out the tip of the strongest shoot at about 1m (3ft) from the ground. Remove any other shoots that come from the base. In the first summer, tie in two good sideshoots at 45 degrees to the wires and

Pruning young wisteria

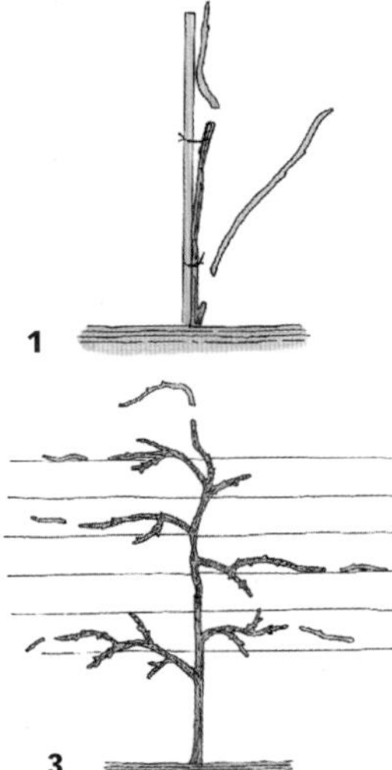

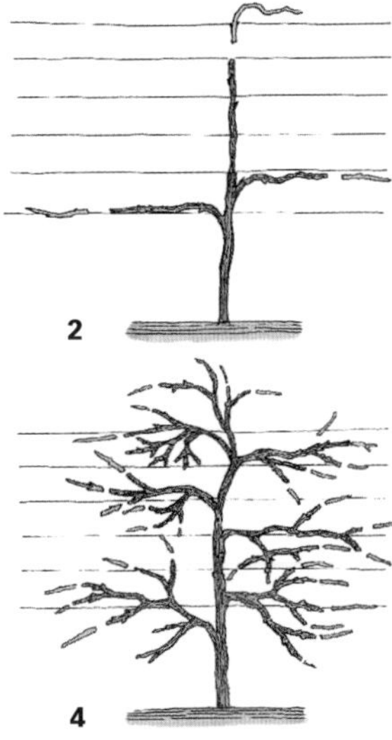

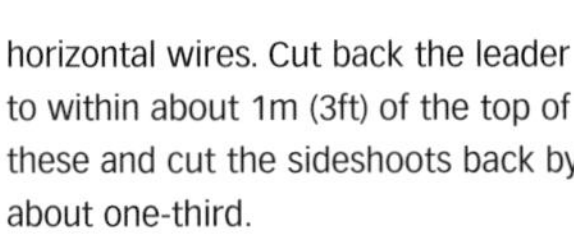

1 In the first winter, cut back the strongest shoot to about 1m (3ft) and remove other shoots.

2 In the first summer, tie in two sideshoots at 45 degrees to the wires and remove other shoots. In the following winter, pull down and the sideshoots and tie them to horizontal wires. Cut back the leader to within about 1m (3ft) of the top of these and cut the sideshoots back by about one-third.

3 Repeat the process in the following year, and continue until the top of the leading shoot is at the height that you desire. Continue to reduce all the sideshoots by about one-third.

4 In subsequent winters, continue to form new horizontal tiers of shoots. Cut back sideshoots to 8–10cm (3–4in).

the leading stem to a vertical cane. Remove all other shoots. In the following winter, pull down and tie the two sideshoots so that they are now horizontal. Cut the leader to within about 1m (3ft) of the top of these and also cut the sideshoots back by about one-third. In the next summer, again tie in the leader to the cane and the next two sideshoots that develop to the wires, again at angles of 45 degrees. Cut back any shoots on the horizontals back to about 15–20cm (6–8in). In winter, pull the two new sideshoots down to the horizontal and tie them down. Reduce the new growth on all horizontals by one-third and cut back the leader to about 1m (3ft) above the top horizontals. Continue with this regime until all the required horizontal sideshoots have been developed.

Once the framework of branches is in position, allow the horizontals to grow, cutting back the new growth by one-third each year until the spread is complete and the available space is covered by the plant.

When this has been achieved, the following routine should be adopted. Each year in late summer, cut back all new growth to about 15cm (6in) or four to six leaves of the older stem. In winter, prune these back even further, to two or three buds, or 8–10cm (3–4in). Once the wisteria is mature, these two simple prunings are all that is required.

Damage to walls and gutters

All climbers, even wisteria, can develop shoots that get behind gutters and lift tiles. However, if climbers are checked every year, few buildings will be damaged. The problems usually arise when either the house or the climber, or both, are neglected. Do not allow self-supporting plants, like ivies, to clamber up painted, pebble-dashed walls. When a surface needs maintenance or to be repainted it is far easier to remove a wooden trellis than to have to pull the climber away from the wall. Many gardeners prefer to grow climbers over garden walls, pergolas or free-stranding trellises, where they cannot damage the fabric of the house.

I would love to have a wisteria in my garden but do not have a suitable wall or pergola. Is it possible to grow wisteria as a standard?

Standard *Wisteria floribunda* (Japanese wisteria)

Although wisteria are usually trained over pergolas or against house walls, it is possible to train a single stem up a stake about 2.1m (7ft) high and to train the branches over a wooden framework that radiates from the stake and forms a flat-topped umbrella.

Start with a young plant and tie it to the stake. Train the shoot's tip upwards and at the same time allow sideshoots to develop; cut them back to about 23cm (9in). When the central shoot is about 45cm (18in) above the top of the supporting framework, cut it off and allow sideshoots at the top to develop to form a canopy. Cut off all other sideshoots close to the main stem. When it is established, both winter and summer pruning will be necessary to ensure the production of flowers as well as to curb excessive growth.

Roses

Rosa 'Evelyn Fison'

Basic techniques

I love roses but worry about pruning them. How do I go about it?
Like all aspects of pruning, roses appear to be daunting at first, but once you have got the hang of it they are relatively easy. The main problem is that there are several groups of roses, each of which is treated in a different way. The first step, therefore, is to identify what type of rose you have got. Keep a note of the name when you buy roses or, if you have lost it or never knew, see if you can find it in one of the many books on roses. Even if you cannot give a name to your rose, it is usually not too difficult to work out what type of rose it is, which is the important thing.

I have seen some roses trained on hooped sticks. What are these?
Roses, in keeping with many shrubs, produce more flowering buds at the top of their stems; if these stems are curved over in an arc, flowerbuds will form along the top of the arc, producing more buds on each stem. Some gardeners tie in the long stems to hazel or other flexible sticks that have had both ends pushed into the soil to form a semicircular hoop. These sticks are arranged all around the bush and all branches are tied down to them. This technique produces a mass of blooms, but not all gardeners like it as they consider that it puts the bush into a straitjacket rather than leaving it as a flowing bush.

Poor pruning cuts

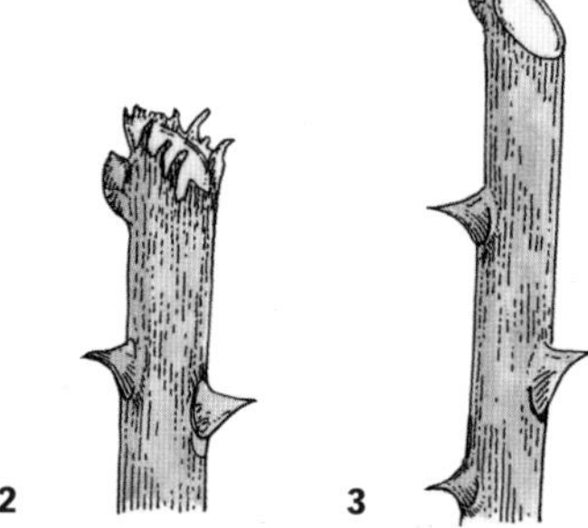

Pruning cuts on roses are made individually with sharp secateurs. Take care that you do not leave short stubs at the plant's base, which are not only unsightly but can cause disease. Cuts should be made just above an outward-facing bud and should slope down slightly. Incorrect pruning cuts are:

1 too far above the bud, leading to die-back;

2 caused by using blunt secateurs; and

3 too close to the bud.

I have been told that you can prune roses simply by shearing them over with either a chainsaw or hedge-trimmers. Is this true?

Yes. Research has shown that some types of roses grow perfectly well if you hack them off just above the ground without thought to precise pruning cuts. However, in spite of this research, most gardeners prefer a more systematic approach and believe a better rose garden will be achieved by following traditional procedures. The disadvantage of using a chainsaw or hedge trimmers is that the plant can look untidy until it regrows.

Removing rose suckers

Rose suckers

Most modern shrub roses are grafted on to a different rootstock, and occasionally suckers appear from the rootstock. If they are simply cut away with secateurs, the sucker will regrow. Try to dig around the rose to find where the sucker arises from the root: pull it cleanly away. The theory is that pulling the sucker away, rather than cutting it, will damage the root, which will be unlikely to regrow. Do not hoe or fork carelessly around roses; this might damage the roots, which encourages suckers to develop.

Species and miniature roses

Rosa 'Anna Ford'

I have several miniature roses around my patio. Do they need pruning?
In spite of their small size – they can reach 30–60cm (1–2ft) high – these roses need to be pruned to give of their best. They flower on the current year's growth and so are similar to a hybrid tea in this respect (see pages 78–9). At the end of flowering, cut back the flowering stems, removing any of the softer, more flexible growth. For the late-winter pruning, remove completely any dead, diseased, dying or damaged shoots. Also make sure you remove any weak growth. Next, cut back the shoots that remain to a strong, outward-facing bud, removing between one-third and a half of the wood. In addition, reduce any laterals to just two or three buds.

Patio roses are sometimes known as dwarf cluster-flowered bush roses, and require similar pruning. The main stems and sideshoots should be cut back by between a half and one-third, and overgrown plants can be renewed by cutting out about one-third of the stems to the base every year for three years.

Rosa pimpinellifolia 'Hispida'

Some species roses

- *Rosa ecae*
- *R. glauca*
- *R. moyesii*
- *R. nitida*
- *R. pendulina*
- *R. pimpinellifolia*
- *R. primula*
- *R. sericea*
- *R. villosa*
- *R. virginiana*

I prefer species roses to modern hybrids, but how do I prune them?
There is little that needs doing to species roses, apart from the usual removal of dead, dying, damaged or diseased wood and any misplaced stems. If the plant becomes congested, it is a good idea to remove some of the older stems from the centre, but other than that there is little to do. Because they also tend to be relatively disease-free, this makes them one of the easiest groups to grow. The down side is that they usually only flower once and can get quite large, taking up a lot of garden space. Several of the species have produced cultivars or close hybrids, such as *Rosa xanthina* 'Canary Bird', *R. rugosa* 'Alba' and *R.* 'Cantabrigiensis', and these are treated in the same way.

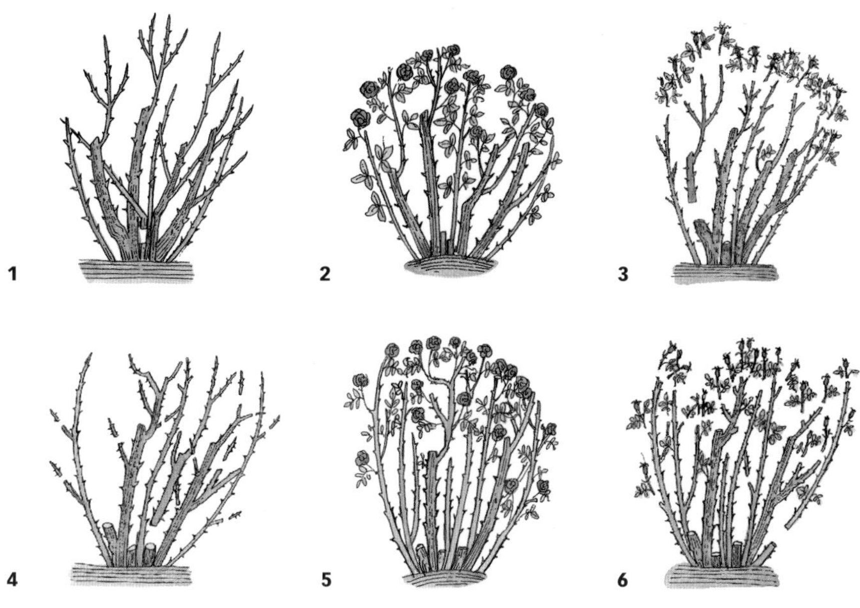

1 In late winter or early spring of the second year, completely cut off shoots that have developed from the base and are badly positioned. Also, cut back the tips of vigorous shoots.

2 In the subsequent summer, the plant will produce flowers on shoots borne on old wood. At the same time, strong, new shoots will develop directly from the shrub's base.

3 In early autumn of the same year, after the flowers have faded, cut out thin and weak growths, as well as those that may be damaged or diseased. Also, cut back the tip of each shoot.

4 In the third and subsequent years, regular pruning in late winter or early spring should include the cutting back of lateral shoots. Also, cut out at their bases one or two old shoots.

5 In mid- and late summer of the same year, the shrub will bear flowers on lateral shoots that have developed on the old shoots. In the same summer, fresh shoots will grow from the base.

6 In early autumn, cut back the tips of shoots to encourage the development of laterals that will bear flowers in the following year.

Rosa 'Silver Jubilee'

Hybrid teas and floribundas

I have just bought a 'Silver Jubilee' rose. How should I prune it?

This is a hybrid tea (large-flowered) rose, and it is in a group that includes some of the most popular garden roses. The initial pruning should be done in the late winter after planting. Cut back all the stems to about 15cm (6in) from the ground to a strong, outward-facing bud. New shoots will develop and these will flower from summer onwards. Remove any flowers as they fade. At the end of flowering, cut back the flowering stems, removing any of the softer, more flexible growth. In late winter, prune out any dead, dying, diseased or crossing stems. Also remove any weak growth. Next cut back the remaining shoots to a strong, outward-facing bud about 23cm (9in) from the ground. Continue this regime of cutting back the flowering stems in autumn and harder pruning in late winter. As the bush gets older, remove one or two of the old stems completely to encourage new growth. This is the type of bush that can be cut back, if you really want to, by chainsaw (see page 75), when you can cut it to 23–25cm (9–10in) from the ground.

I have bought what is called a floribunda rose. How do I prune it?

Floribunda (cluster-flowered) roses produce clusters of flowers over a long period from summer into autumn. Although they are more vigorous plants than hybrid teas, they should not be pruned as hard because it will weaken them. The initial pruning is the same as with the hybrid teas: cut back the new plant late in its first winter to about 25cm (10in). After flowering, cut back the flowering tips to a convenient point. At the end of the following winter, remove the usual dead, dying, damaged or diseased wood, along with any weak or crossing stems. Prune the remaining stems by about one-third and cut back any sideshoots to 12–15cm (5–6in). The shrub should now be mature. From now on, cut back the flowering tips in autumn, and in late winter take out all the dead and diseased wood. Consider the remaining framework and cut out one or two of the oldest stems to 15–20cm (6–8in), pruning the remaining ones back by about one-third and any remaining sideshoots to about 15cm (6in). If the bush becomes crowded as it ages, take out one or two of the oldest stems right to the base. Continue these last two steps every year.

Preparatory pruning

Whether you are pruning hybrid tea or floribunda bush roses, the initial task is the same.

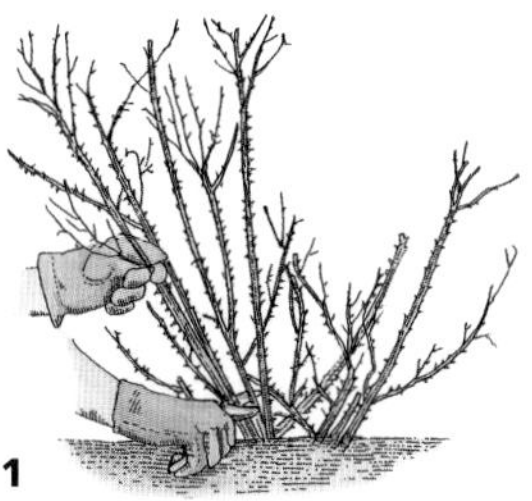

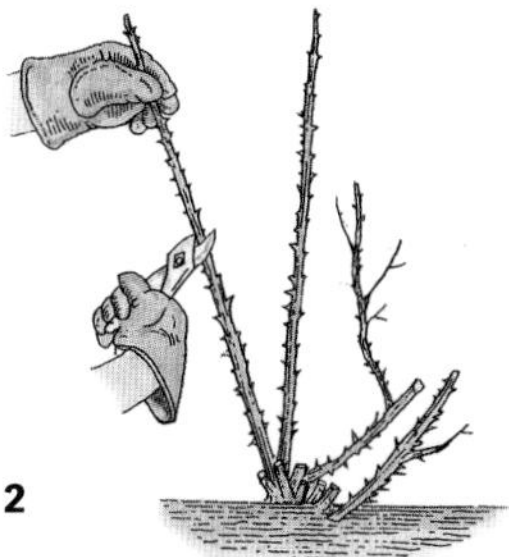

1 Cut out dead wood at the base and remove shoots that are rubbing against each other. Also cut out those infected by disease. If the cut surface is brown, the stem is infected and a lower cut is needed where the wood is white.

2 Cut out thin, weak and spindly shoots to their bases. Make sure that the centre is open so air can circulate, which helps shoots to ripen, enabling them to resist the entry of diseases. Prune remaining stems by one-third.

3 The shoots that remain should all be strong and healthy and make a well-spaced framework.

Pruning techniques

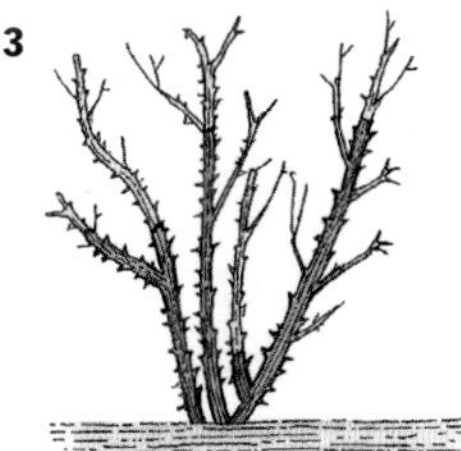

1 In **hard pruning**, sometimes called low pruning, stems are cut back to three or four buds, leaving stems 13–15cm (5–6in) long. This method is suitable for newly planted hybrid tea and floribunda roses as it encourages strong shoots to develop from the plant's base. It is not suitable for most established bush roses, although weak-growing hybrid teas are frequently hard pruned, and it is a method that is often used to rejuvenate neglected hybrid teas, but not established floribundas.

2 In **moderate, or medium, pruning**, stems are cut back by about half their length, although weak ones need more severe treatment. This approach is ideal for most hybrid tea and floribunda roses, especially those that are growing in ordinary soil. If, after a few years, hybrid tea types have become too high and leggy, prune hard in one season.

3 In **light pruning**, sometimes known as high or long pruning, the top one-third of all shoots is removed. The approach is often used on vigorous hybrid tea roses, because it does not encourage the further growth of strong shoots, and restricts the plant's height. It is the ideal method for all bush roses growing in sandy soils, where the fertility is low and therefore insufficient to provide the vigorous growth encouraged by hard pruning.

Shrub roses

How do I prune old-fashioned shrub roses?

There are two types of shrub rose: those that flower once a year and those that are repeat-flowering. Most old-fashioned roses only flower once, and it is these that we consider here. The group includes albas, damasks, centifolias and mosses, and a few modern roses that flower only once. The flowers are borne on sideshoots produced from the older wood, so hard pruning is not required or the plant will never flower.

Initial pruning after planting is restricted to removing any shoots that have become damaged. After flowering, the old flowering shoots are shortened slightly by removing the flowering tips so that the wind does not damage the plant in winter. In late winter or early spring, the main pruning is to prevent the shrub becoming too large and leggy. To do this, cut back all the new basal growth from the previous year by about one-third. On the older stems, cut back all sideshoots and sub-sideshoots to 10–13cm (4–5in). When the shrub begins to get a bit crowded, cut out one or two of the older stems right back to the base. All dead, dying, diseased and crossing wood should also be removed as a matter of course.

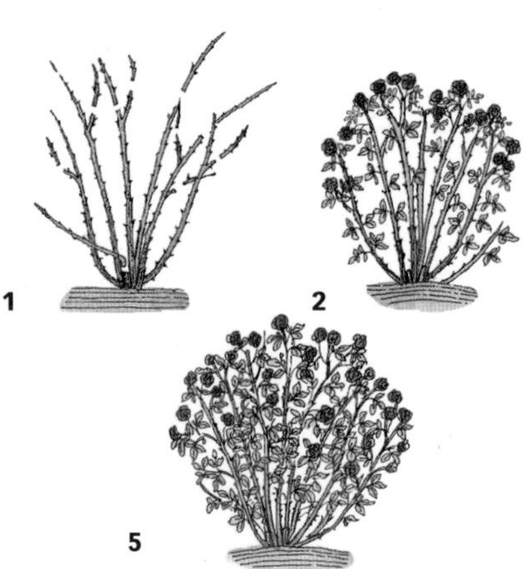

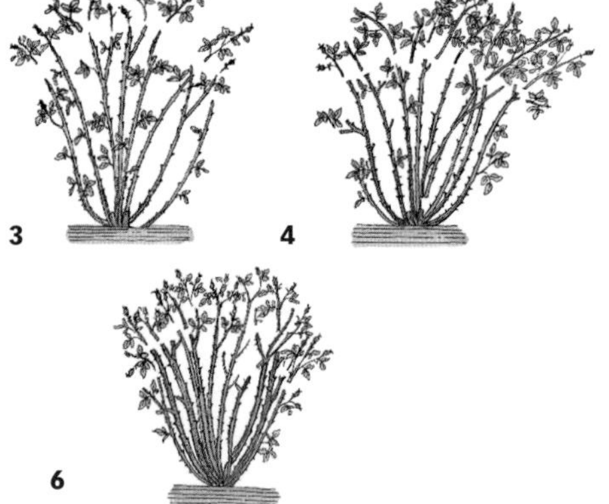

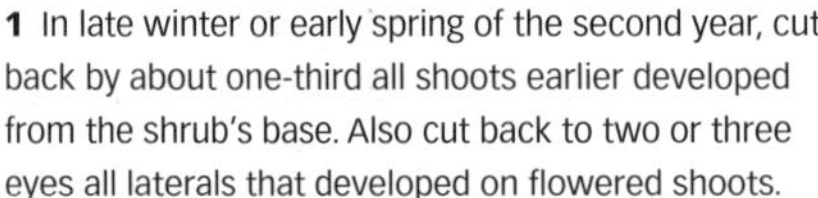

1 In late winter or early spring of the second year, cut back by about one-third all shoots earlier developed from the shrub's base. Also cut back to two or three eyes all laterals that developed on flowered shoots.

2 From mid- to late summer of the second year, flowers will be borne on lateral shoots that were cut back earlier. Cut off the flowers as they fade.

3 From early to late autumn of the second year, cut back any long shoots to prevent plant damage or loosening of roots caused by autumn and winter winds.

4 In late winter and early spring of the third and subsequent years, cut back by one-third new shoots that developed from ground level. Also cut back laterals on flowered shoots to two or three eyes, and cut out a few old shoots at the base.

5 From mid- to late summer of the same year, the bush will bear flowers on lateral shoots that were cut back earlier. The cycle of fresh shoots growing each year and later developing sideshoots that will bear flowers is repeated the following season.

6 In early to late autumn, cut off the ends of long stems to reduce the area of stems and help to prevent the shrub's roots being disturbed when shoots are blown by strong winds in autumn and winter.

I have an old-fashioned shrub rose. It never seems to flower well in spite of being pruned hard each year. What should I do?

The problem is that most old-fashioned shrub roses flower only on sideshoots produced by old wood. If you prune the rose hard, you will be removing that old wood and not giving the plant time to flower because it will be constantly producing non-flowering new wood. Let the shrub grow for a year and follow the instructions given opposite.

I have started to collect modern shrub roses. How should I prune them?

Most modern shrub roses, including the popular English roses, are repeat-flowering. The few that are not should be treated in the same way as the once-flowering, old-fashioned roses (see opposite). Not all of the old-fashioned roses are once-flowering, however; some, such as many of the China roses and the Bourbons, also repeat and are included in this group. They are basically treated as the once-flowering group but, while you can deadhead once-flowering roses to tidy them up if you wish to, it is essential that you deadhead repeat-flowering roses or the bushes will become congested and flowering impaired.

Repeat-flowering shrub roses

The following repeat-flowering roses can be pruned as outlined below left.

- 'Abraham Darby'
- 'Cardinal Hume'
- 'Charles Austin'
- 'Cymbeline'
- 'Evelyn'
- 'Jacqueline du Pré'
- 'Märchenland'
- 'Marguerite Hilling'
- 'Nevada'
- 'The Squire'

***Rosa* 'The Squire'**

Once-flowering, old-fashioned roses

These roses are pruned as described above:

- 'Alba Maxima'
- 'Céleste'
- 'Fantin-Latour'
- 'Félicité Parmentier'
- 'Henri Martin'
- 'Königen von Dänemark'
- 'Madame Hardy'
- 'Robert le Diable'
- 'Shailer's White Moss'
- 'Willam Lobb'

***Rosa* 'Madame Hardy'**

Standard *Rosa* 'Excelsa'

Standard roses

I would love to have a standard rose but am worried about keeping its shape. Is it difficult to prune?

Although you can graft your own standards, I would be inclined to buy one already growing on its tall stem. They are readily available from specialist rose nurseries and garden centres. What you have in effect is a bush rose growing on the top of a single straight stem, very similar to a tree trunk. This type of rose is exactly the same as the equivalent bush rose and is treated in exactly the same way, depending on its category. Thus if you have a standard 'Peace' rose you would prune the bushy part on the top of the stem as you would an ordinary hybrid tea. In fact, to keep them compact it is a good idea to prune them slightly harder, so stems that are usually cut back to 15cm (6in) would be cut back to, say, 10cm (4in). There should be no need to do any pruning on the main stem, but ensure that it is well supported by a strong stake and a good-quality tie.

Standard roses

There are four basic types of standard rose. Heights vary according to grower.

- Ordinary standard rose, which is usually about 1.15m (45in) high.
- Bush standards are similar, about 1.2m (4ft) high.
- Half-standards are usually about 75cm (30in) high, a height that is useful for small gardens or containers; they are pruned in the same way as normal standard roses.
- Weeping standards have weeping foliage. These are usually grafted at 1.5m (5ft) and are treated as described right.

Pruning techniques

1 In late winter or early spring after planting, cut back strong stems on hybrid tea roses to three to four eyes of their bases. With floribundas, cut stems to six to eight eyes.

2 In the following autumn or early winter, cut off the flowerheads and completely remove soft, unripe and thin shoots. This reduces the risk of wind damaging the standard's head in early winter.

3 In late winter and early spring of the following year, cut out dead, weak and diseased shoots. Also cut out any crossing shoots.

4 Cut new shoots on hybrid teas to three to five eyes, and laterals to two to four. With floribundas, cut new shoots to six to eight eyes and laterals to three to six eyes.

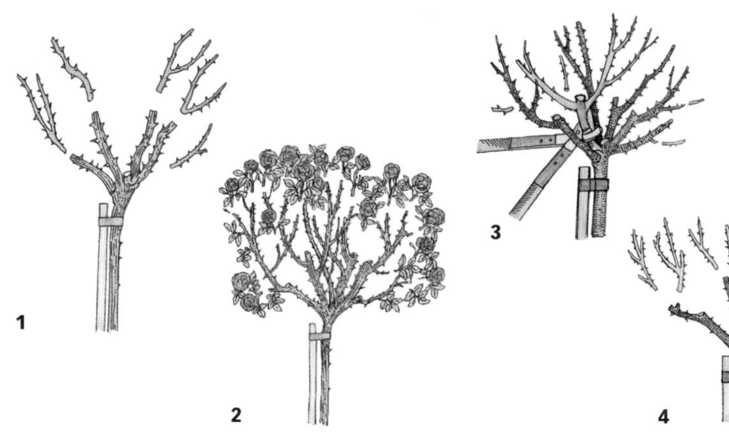

Weeping standards

This popular form of standard rose has a cascading, weeping appearance. They are mainly produced by budding rambler varieties on 1.2–1.8m (4–6ft) tall stems of Rosa rugosa. Pruning is simple. In late summer or early autumn, completely cut out two-year-old shoots that have flowers. This will leave young shoots that developed earlier in summer to produce flowers in the following year. If there are insufficient young stems to replace the old ones that are cut out, leave a few of these older ones and cut back any lateral shoots on them to two or three eyes. Make sure the main stem is secured to a stake.

Rosa 'Golden Showers'

Climbing roses

I love climbing roses but am rather afraid of pruning them in case I spoil them. What should I do?

There are two groups of climbers: first there are the climbing roses themselves, and then there are the rambling roses. Although they look similar and are often difficult to tell apart at a casual glance, they are pruned in different ways, and the first task is to find out which group your plants are in. If you do not know the name, the easiest way of telling them apart is that the ramblers produce more new growth from the base than climbers do. See page 87 for how to prune ramblers.

Climbers should not be pruned for the first two years, although any stems or shoots that die back should be cut out. They should be trained by tying in the stems to a framework; tying them in horizontally or in a low arch will promote maximum flowering as well as helping to cover the available space.

After two or three years, you can start pruning. Climbers can be left unpruned, but they will eventually become a tangled mass that can be difficult to deal with without drastic action. If climbers are allowed to climb up through large trees they can be left to their own devices, but in most gardens, where they are grown against the side of a house, for example, it is best to do a little pruning every autumn after flowering. Shorten the sideshoots and tie them in to the framework, again tying them horizontally if possible. It is also a good idea to remove one or possibly two of the oldest main stems, to make room for the new growth as well as to encourage new stems to rise from the base of the plant.

Pruning climbers

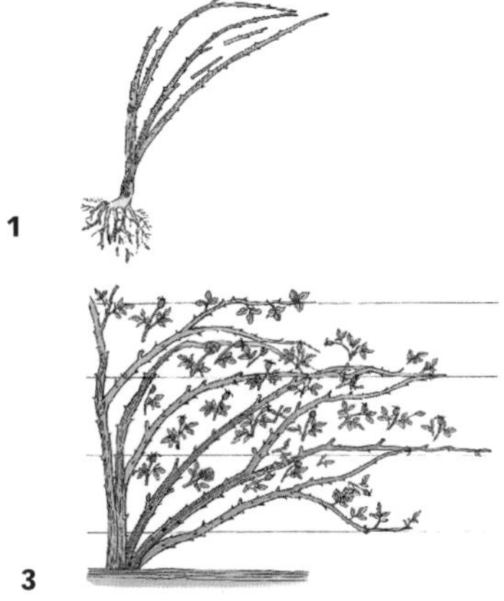

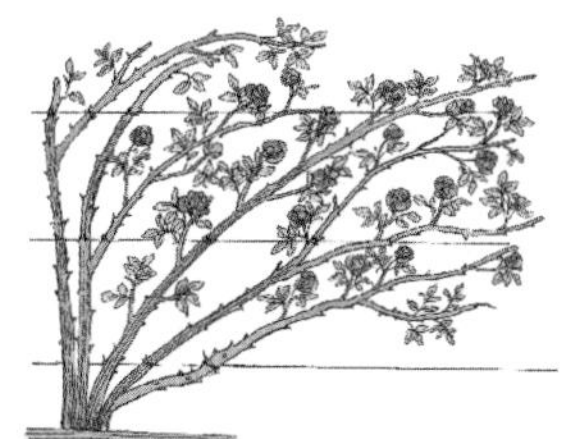

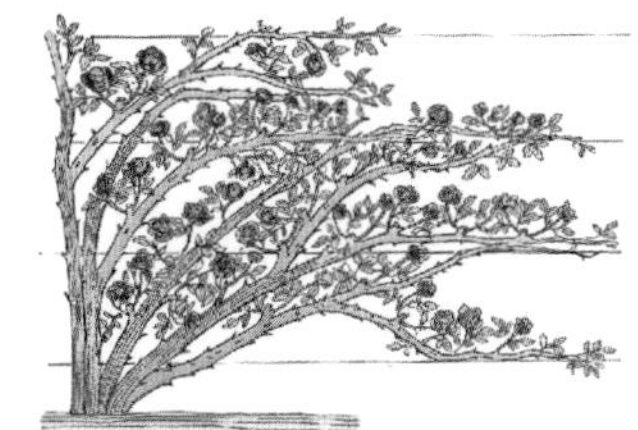

1 When a climber is first planted, cut back coarse and uneven roots. Also cut out weak shoots at the bases and lightly cut back the tips of unripe and damaged shoots. Loosely tie in the stems to create a permanent framework.

2 In mid- and late summer of the following season, tie in new shoots that develop from the existing framework and that grow from ground level.

3 From between mid-autumn of the same year and early spring of the following year, cut back all lateral shoots that have borne flowers to within three or four eyes of their points of origin. Cut out weak and diseased shoots and tie in leading shoots to the framework. Thin and weak shoots arising from the climber's base should also be cut out. If pruning is left until early spring, also cut out frost-damaged shoots.

4 In the following mid- and late summer, flowers are borne on the tips of new growths as well as on lateral shoots. When the flowers fade, cut them off. Also tie in new shoots as they grow. Later in the same season, from mid-autumn to early spring, cut back all lateral shoots that have borne flowers to three or four eyes of their point of origin. Cut out weak and diseased shoots.

Climbing roses

Roses that have the word 'Climbing' in front of their name – 'Climbing Iceberg', for example – are climbing forms of bush roses, and if they are heavily pruned during their first two or three years they may revert to a bush form and never produce the long stems that are required of a true climber or rambler.

Rosa **'Climbing Iceberg'**

Are pillar roses climbers? How do I prune them?

Pillar roses can be regarded as a type of climbing rose. They have an upright growth, but rarely get much higher than about 3m (10ft). Their upright habit and limited height make them ideal for growing up posts or pillars. The roses are borne on sideshoots on older growth. Remove any damaged stems on planting and tie in the shoots to the pillar. After flowering, remove the old flowerheads. In autumn, remove any dead, damaged or diseased wood and cut back any excessive growth both on the leaders and sideshoots. As the plant gets older, remove one or two of the older stems to the base.

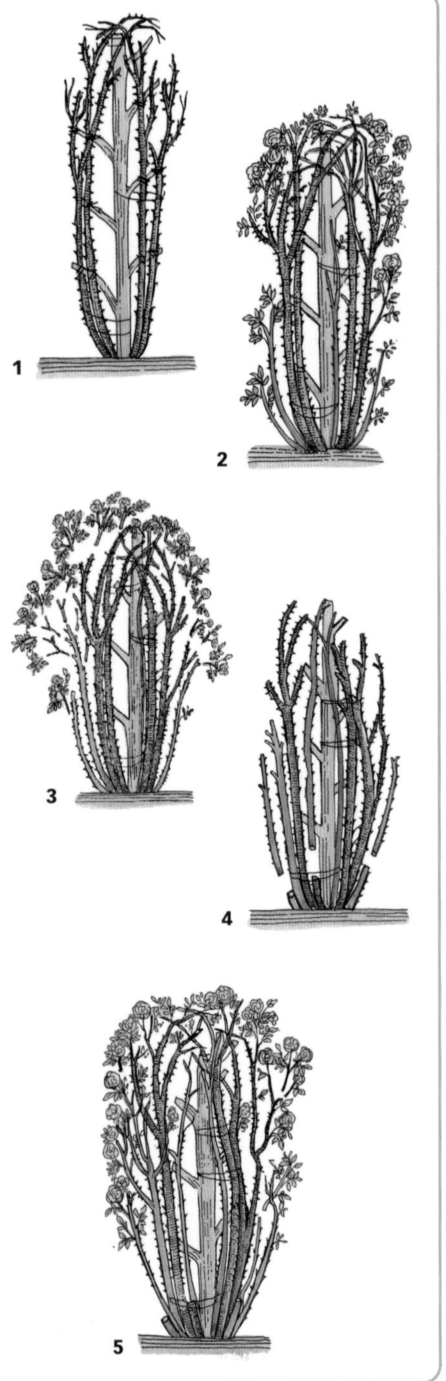

1 In the first summer after being planted, pillar roses develop long stems. Train these in upright and secure them to a pole.

2 In the following summer, the plant bears flowers on small, lateral shoots that have grown on the long stems that developed in the previous year. In summer, fresh, long shoots develop from the plant's base. Cut off all flowers as they fade to keep the plant tidy, removing the complete flower truss.

3 In late autumn or early winter of the same year, cut back all lateral shoots that developed flowers. Prune back some of the young shoots produced in the year. Ensure they are spread evenly around the plant, not clustered on the sunny side.

4 Also in late autumn or early winter of the same year, cut out weak shoots that have developed from the plant's base. Also remove diseased and dead wood and totally cut out a few of the oldest shoots. Repeat the cycle of cutting out old stems and training in new ones each year; if this is neglected, the plant will become a mass of tangled shoots that produce few flowers.

5 In the following and subsequent years, lateral shoots on the previous year's growth will bear flowers in summer. Cut these off as they fade. In late autumn or early winter of the same year, cut out all laterals that produced flowers.

Rambling roses

What is the difference between ramblers and climbers and how does this affect the pruning?

Ramblers produce a lot more new growth from the base than climbers. A number of the old stems may also die after flowering, and unripe wood may also die back in winter. Ramblers should be pruned in late summer or autumn after flowering. If you have room, the best way of coping with a rambler is to untie it and spread it out on the ground. Cut out any dead wood to the base and unripe wood back to good wood. Remove up to a third of the old wood right back to the base. Reduce any sideshoots to between two and four buds. Some gardeners prefer to remove all stems on which flowers were produced and leave only the new growth. Retrain the remaining shoots onto their supports, tying them in as near to the horizontal as possible.

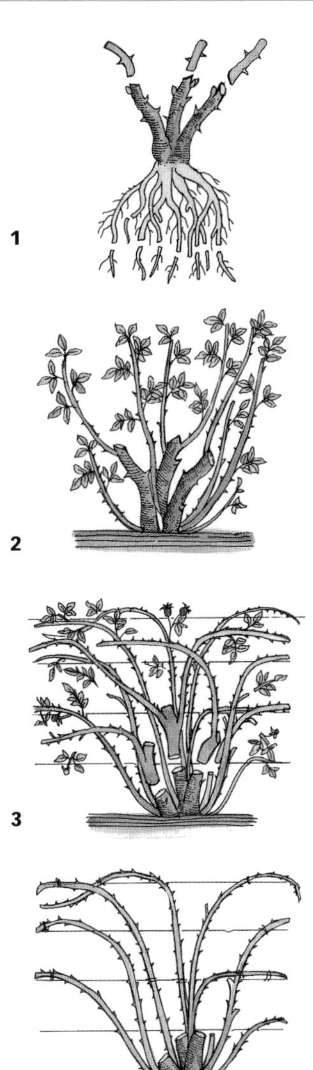

1 Plant a new rambler between late autumn and early spring. Cut back coarse, unevenly long roots. The rose will have three or four stems, each to 1.2m (4ft) long. Cut these back to 23–38cm (9–15in), then plant it firmly in good, well-drained soil.

2 In spring, young shoots will develop from buds at the top of each stem. These will form the initial flowering stems and framework, although the aim must eventually be to encourage fresh shoots to develop from the plant's base each and every year.

3 In late summer or autumn thereafter, cut out flowered shoots to their bases, leaving, tying in and spacing out on supports all strong shoots that developed earlier that season. Take care not to damage these shoots by tying them too tightly.

4 At the same time, cut back all shoots that are growing from these main ones to within two or three eyes of their base. Rejuvenate neglected ramblers by cutting all shoots back. Although this means losing the following season's flowers, it is the best way to restore regular flowering.

Tree Fruit

'Gala' apples

Apples and pears: basic techniques

What is the difference between apples and pears?

Apples (*Malus domestica*) and pears (*Pyrus communis*) are the most popular tree fruits in temperate regions, each year reliably producing large crops. Pears develop their blossom slightly earlier in a season than apples and therefore are more likely to be damaged by late spring frosts. Consequently, they benefit from a warm, sheltered position. Because they flower before apples, the summer pruning of pears takes place about a week earlier than it does for apples. Otherwise, the pruning of both fruits is similar, although during a tree's formative period pears are best pruned less vigorously. Once they start to bear fruit, pear trees can be pruned more severely than apples, both when cutting back the tips of leading shoots and when shortening lateral ones. Indeed, pears develop fruit spurs more readily than apples, with the result that more attention should be given in subsequent years to thinning them out. If thinning is neglected, the fruit will eventually be small and of poor quality.

Is there more than one type of apple tree?

Yes, apple trees can be grown in a variety of ways, mainly depending on the shape of the tree but sometimes also on its size, which is largely determined by the rootstock on which the plant is grown. The rootstock controls the vigour of the tree, and when you buy an apple (or pear) tree it is important to know what stock it is on. Standard trees, for example, need a more vigorous stock than a dwarf pyramid, and it would be pointless trying to train the former

Apple rootstocks

Those marked with an asterisk (*) are suitable for normal garden use.

M27*	Extreme dwarfing stock	Bush, dwarf pyramid, cordon
M9*	Dwarfing stock	Bush, dwarf pyramid, cordon
M26*	Semi-dwarfing stock	Bush, dwarf pyramid, cordon
MM106*	Semi-dwarfing stock	Bush, spindle bush, cordon, fan, espalier
M7	Semi-dwarfing stock	Bush, spindle bush, cordon, fan, espalier
M4	Semi-vigorous stock	Bush, spindle bush
MM4	Vigorous stock	Standard
M2	Vigorous stock	Standard
MM111*	Vigorous stock	Half-standard, standard, large bush, large fan, large espalier
M25	Vigorous stock	Standard
MM109	Vigorous stock	Standard
M1	Vigorous stock	Standard

as if it were the latter. Your choice of the size and shape of the tree will depend on how much space you have in your garden: you can fit many cordon apples into the space that would be covered by a full standard apple tree, for example. On the other hand, a standard apple tree provides wonderful dappled shade, which is something a cordon can never give.

The main types of apple tree are dwarf pyramid, bush, spindle bush, half-standard, standard, cordon, espalier and fan. Pears are usually grown as standards, half-standards, bushes, cordons, dwarf pyramids, espaliers or fans. Pears are normally grown on a quince rootstock for the smaller trees and on a pear stock for the more vigorous standards and half-standards, which are really only suitable for growing in larger gardens.

I have a small garden but would love a pear tree. What is the best method?

Pears are treated in largely the same way as apples. Cordons probably take up least space, and it is possible to have, say, two pears and even three or four apples in a relatively small space. Pear cordons are pruned in the same way as apple cordons (see pages 100–101). If you want a more conventional-looking tree, a dwarf pyramid is the most suitable for a small garden, although you may prefer a bush. For decorative effect you could also grow pears as espaliers, perhaps against a fence. Again, these methods are the same as for apples (see pages 102–3). Make sure the tree you choose is grown on an appropriate rootstock.

Pear blossom always looks attractive. Is it possible to train a tree into an arch to make a decorative feature of this?

Yes. Pears can be trained to form an arch, and it can look beautiful when in blossom, and all year round, including autumn when the foliage of some varieties takes on fiery colours. They are not difficult to train. Start with a metal arch to act as a former. If you make a wooden arch, it can be removed once the pears have become firmly established and they will hold their shape. Ideally, use an arch with a curved top. Train one or more pears up each side of the arch, treating them as cordons (see pages 100–101).

Formative pruning

➡ What is a standard tree and how do I achieve it?

Half-standard apple tree

A standard tree is a conventional-looking tree. Full standards can be large and need tall ladders to reach the fruit. Half-standards are more suitable for most gardens. The tree has a clear trunk that reaches to 2.1m (7ft) for a full standard and 1.2–1.35m (4–4½ft) for a half-standard before the branches start.

The purpose of training and pruning is to produce a well-balanced head of branches with an open centre, which allows air and light to get to all the fruit. Choose a young tree on suitable stock and plant it in winter. Generally the same procedures are followed as for an open-centred bush (see below). Because the tree is larger, it will support a few more main branches, up to say five. Try to keep the centre of the tree open so that plenty of light gets in to ripen the fruit.

➡ I have been offered a feathered maiden apple tree. What is it?

A feathered maiden is a young tree that is one year old and already has several sideshoots. Most apple trees are supplied from nurseries in this form. Sometimes the tree is bought as a maiden whip, which consists of a leader and no sideshoots. To obtain sideshoots on a maiden whip, cut back the leader by about half its length to a good bud.

➡ What is a bush apple tree and how is it pruned?

A bush is a compromise between a full-grown apple tree and a dwarf tree. It is suitable for a medium-sized garden and is usually grown with an open centre, which is created when the leader is removed. The leader is left on a spindle bush so that a taller bush results. If it is left unpruned, an open-centred bush is likely to revert to growing a leader and become taller. Plant the new tree in winter as a feathered maiden and cut back the leader to about 75cm (30in) from the ground. Cut it to a strong sideshoot. Choose three well-spaced, strong laterals and remove the rest. Cut the remaining three back to one-third of their original length to a strong, upward-facing bud. In the following winter, remove completely any growth that is crossing the centre of the bush. Choose a few strong growths that are suitable for continuing the development of the branch framework and reduce these by about half. Cut back any other shoots to three or four buds. Repeat this the following winter, by which time the shape of the bush should be firmly established. From now on, it is a matter of spur-pruning (see pages 95–7) to promote good fruiting and to keep the bush compact.

Formative pruning for a bush

1

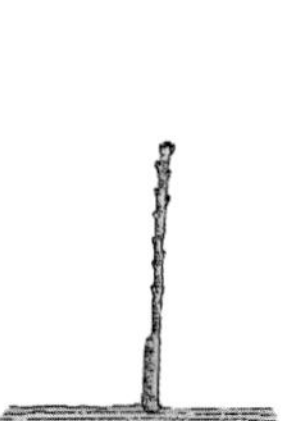
2

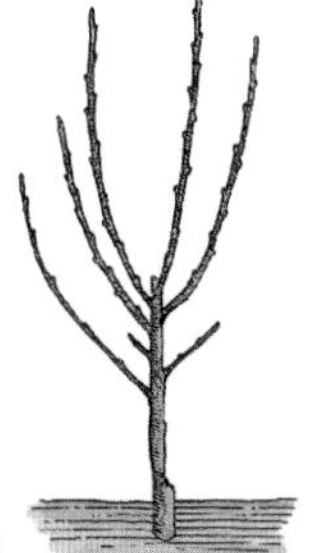
3

4

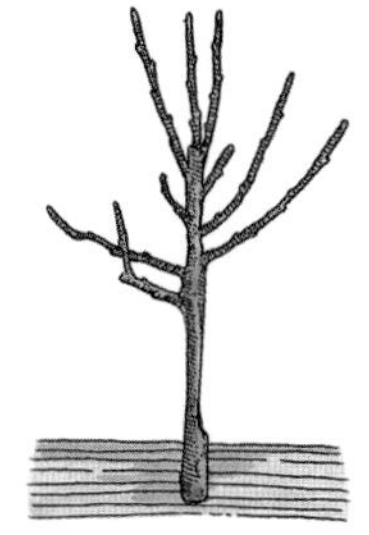
5

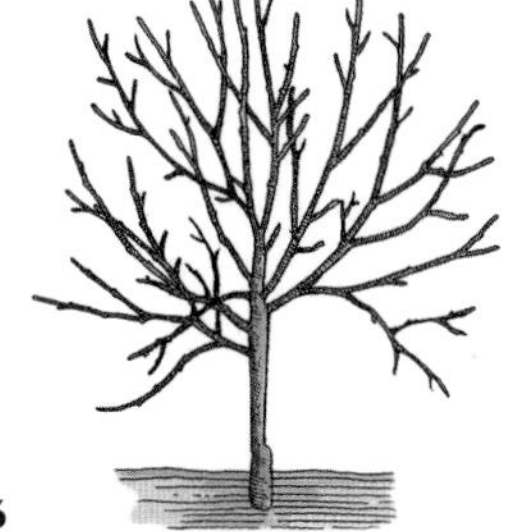
6

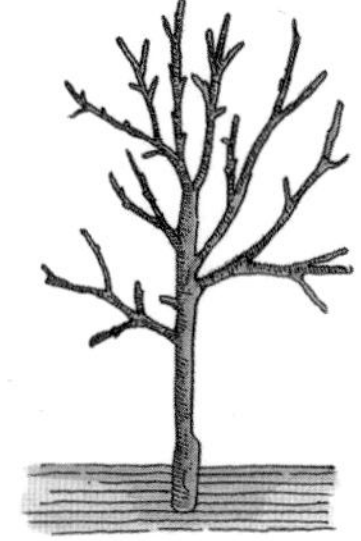
7

1 Plant a bare-rooted, one-year-old tree (maiden) in winter. This will have a single stem without any sideshoots. Take care not to knock or excessively strain the graft or the area around it.

2 Prune the one-year-old tree in winter whenever the air temperature is above freezing. Create a dwarf bush by cutting the stem back to 60cm (2ft) above ground level, severing just above a healthy bud. When an ordinary bush is required, cut 75cm (30in) above soil level.

3 By the following winter, the plant will have developed several strong stems that grow upwards. The bush should have shoots that form wide angles with the main stem, and some shoots will be growing from lower down on the stem.

4 Select four strong, well-spaced shoots to form the main framework and cut them back by two-thirds. Prune each to just above a healthy, outward-facing bud. Cut out all unwanted shoots flush with the main stem.

5 In winter, cut back all leading shoots by about two-thirds of their length. Cut out damaged shoots, as well as those that cross the top of the bush. Small lateral shoots should be cut back to three buds to encourage the formation of fruiting spurs.

6 By the following winter, the four-year-old bush will have several leading shoots as well as younger, slender sideshoots. The severity of winter pruning influences the subsequent growth and development of fruit: the greater the proportion of wood removed, the more vigorous the following year's growth will be and the smaller the crop of fruit produced will be.

7 In winter, shorten the leading shoots by one-third to a half, depending on the bush's vigour. Cut back lateral shoots that are growing on the insides of the branches and towards the bush's centre to about 10cm (4in) long. Prune out dead and crossing shoots.

'Wagener' dessert apples grown as a dwarf pyramid

I have been told that dwarf pyramid trees would be ideal for my small garden. How do I prune them?

A dwarf pyramid is a tree about 2.1m (7ft) high. It is grown on a dwarfing stock and is not vigorous. It develops a main stem to the top of the tree and is not open-centred. In the first winter, the leader is pruned to about 75cm (30in) from the ground. All sideshoots are also cut back to about 15cm (6in) from the trunk. In the following summer, all new growth on the tips of sideshoots is cut back to five or six leaves and any sideshoots on them are reduced to three leaves. During the tree's second winter, the new growth on the leader is again reduced, this time to about 25cm (10in). From now, during each summer, continue to cut back the new growth on the main sideshoots to five or six leaves, and that off the new growth on spurs to one leaf. Any new sideshoots on the main shoots should also be reduced to one leaf. In winter, when the leader reaches the required height, cut back the new growth to one bud. Winter pruning should now also become routine for each year, and this consists of thinning any clusters of spurs (see pages 95–7).

What is a spindle bush?

This is a relatively new way of growing apples in which the main growth is restricted to three or four branches. The leader is left intact and allowed to grow to a preferred height. Below this and above the main branches, new branches are allowed to grow each year, but once they have fruited they are removed. The main branches are often pulled down until they are nearly horizontal and tied down with string fastened to pegs in the ground. This stops them from becoming too vigorous as well as promoting fruiting. A maiden tree is planted in winter, and the main sideshoots are reduced to three or four strong growths. These are cut back by about half. The leader is also cut back to a strong bud.

In the first summer, once the main branches have grown, pull these down to an angle of about 30 degrees from the horizontal and tie them with strong string to a peg inserted in the ground. At the same time, cut out any upward-facing sideshoots on these branches. Tie the new leader to an upright stake. In the following winter, reduce the new growth on this leader by about one-third. In the next summer, tie down any upward-facing shoots, removing any excessively vigorous ones.

By the fourth year, the bush will have taken on a good pyramidal shape made up of tiers of branches. From this point, use renewal pruning as the method of pruning (see page 96). Shorten fruited wood and take out completely some of the older sideshoots, particularly towards the top of the tree. Once the wood has hardened, the strings can be removed as the branches will stay in position.

'Doyenné du Comice' pears

Pear varieties

Early varieties:

- 'Beth' (dessert)
- 'Clapp's Favourite' (dessert)
- 'Jargonelle' (dessert)
- 'Williams' Bon Chrétien' (dessert)

Mid-season:

- 'Beurré Clairgeau' (dual purpose)
- 'Beurré Hardy' (dessert)
- 'Concorde' (dessert)
- 'Conference' (dessert)
- 'Doyenné du Comice' (dessert)
- 'Improved Fertility' (dual purpose)
- 'Onward' (dessert)
- 'Pitmaston Duchess' (dual purpose)

Late season:

- 'Beurré Alexandre Lucas' (dessert)
- 'Black Wooster' (culinary)
- 'Catillac' (culinary)
- 'Glou Morceau' (dessert)
- 'Joséphine de Malines' (dessert)
- 'Winter Nelis' (dessert)

'Belle de Soignes' pear tree in blossom

Established tree

I think I have pruned my trees correctly, but they seem to put on a lot of growth and not much fruit. Is this a pruning problem?
It is not a pruning problem in the sense that you may have done something wrong, but pruning may provide the solution. The tree is too vigorous and needs some action to slow it down. The most commonly used method may seem unlikely, but it is to prune the roots rather than the branches. You need to dig a trench around the tree, positioning it under the branches at the widest part of the tree. Tie a string to the trunk of the tree and tie a stick to the other end at the furthest branch spread. Walk in a circle around the tree, keeping the string taut, and mark a circle on the ground. Use this as a guide to dig the trench. It will be quite an effort as it should be about two spades wide and up to 60cm (2ft) deep. Do not sever the fibrous roots, but cut through any thick roots at either side of the trench; remove the resulting sections. Fill in the trench and water the area under the tree thoroughly before applying a mulch. This should curb the vigour of the tree and result in more fruit.

Some gardeners prune their fruit trees in summer and others in winter. Which is correct?
In large-scale orchards, where these fruits are grown as bushes, half-standards and standards, pruning is carried out in winter. In gardens, however, and especially where tree fruits are grown as espaliers and cordons, they are pruned in both winter and summer.

Occasionally, trees that are heavily pruned in summer become infested with woolly aphids. Winter pruning is normally carried out in a tree's dormant period, but it can be delayed and performed after buds begin to swell. The disadvantage of late pruning, however, is that it often checks subsequent growth – although this reaction can sometimes be used to advantage if you have to prune an excessively vigorous tree.

Once a tree's framework and shape are established, specially trained trees, such as cordons and espaliers, can be summer pruned. The removal of shoots and leaves in summer checks the growth of roots and reduces the development of shoots. It also leads to the formation of fruit buds at the base of the shoot that has been pruned. Winter pruning is done to direct the growth of a tree into branch and shoot development; to prevent the overcrowding of branches and lateral shoots; and to regulate the number and position of fruit buds that subsequently develop and produce flowers and fruit.

Pruning an apple tree

How do I spur-prune?

Cut back new sideshoots (laterals) to about four buds in winter to encourage flowerbuds to form. In the following year, cut back the shoot even further to just above the top flowerbud so that any further growth is restricted to producing more flowerbuds on short stems (spurs). Continue to reduce laterals as they appear.

Eventually the spurs will become a tangled mass of zigzagging short shoots. These will need thinning. Prune some of the older spurs back to their base on the stem; thin some of the other clusters. Aim to create evenly spaced spurs. Spur-pruning is not often required because crowding usually occurs only on old trees.

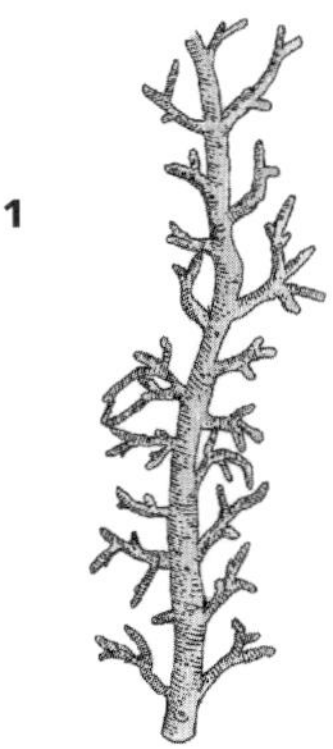

1 A branch with overcrowded spurs.

2 In winter, cut out spurs to make sure they are evenly spaced along each branch.

Apple blossom

What is renewal pruning?

This type of pruning takes into account the fact that some varieties of apple produce blossom on two-year-old wood. The idea is to leave selected sideshoots unpruned; in the following year, these are 'tipped back' to remove the new growth at the end of the shoot as far as the old, which carries the flowerbuds. In the following year, the shoot that has fruited is cut back to 2–3cm (about 1in). A new shoot develops from this, and it is treated in the same way – that is, it is left for the first year and cut back during the second.

What is biennial bearing?

Some apple varieties, such as 'Blenheim Orange', 'Bramley's Seedling' and 'Laxton's Superb', bear a heavier crop in one year than the next. One way to even out this problem is to take action in the spring before a heavy crop is expected. Rub half to three-quarters of the fruit buds from each spur, leaving only one or two fruiting buds on each. Biennial bearing is less of a problem with pears.

'Bramley's Seedling' apples

I have heard some apples described as spur-bearers and some as tip-bearers. Is there a difference and does it matter?

Apart from shape, from the pruning point of view one of the most important characteristics of apple trees is that some cultivars produce fruit on spurs while others produce it on unpruned, two-year-old shoots; these are known as tip-bearers. The spurs are short sideshoots, which end in a flowerbud. They occur all along a shoot and often have a jagged outline. Tip-bearers produce fruit only along the old stems, and this has important implications. For example, cordons or espaliers are pruned hard, and so only spur-bearing trees can be used because a tip-bearer would have all its fruiting potential removed each year by the pruning. To encourage the development of spurs, the technique of spur-pruning is used, and for tip-bearers renewal pruning is used. The majority of apples are spur-pruned.

Pruning spur-bearing trees

1 On an established spur-bearing apple tree, the aim of pruning is to encourage the regular development of spurs along each branch.

2 In winter, shorten lateral shoots to three or four buds from their bases. Shorten to one bud long laterals that were pruned in the previous year. Prune back the leader to half of the growth produced in the previous year, cutting to an upward-facing bud.

What is the best way to thin out spurs and when should this be done?

After several years, branches of varieties that bear their fruit on spurs often become too numerous, forming complicated patterns. Because of the congestion, the quality and size of their fruit diminishes. In winter, completely remove some of the spurs and thin out a few others. Make sure that the remaining spurs are evenly spaced along the branches. As well as concentrating the tree's energies into fewer spurs, this means that more light and air can enter the tree.

What happens if I don't prune my apple tree?

If you do not prune an apple tree, or other fruit tree, it will become very overgrown and tangled. The amount of blossom and, consequently, the amount of fruit will decrease as the tree becomes more congested. In addition, much of the fruit will become damaged as it rubs in the wind against the thicket of branches. The tangle of branches will make it difficult to reach the fruit to harvest it, and fruit will be left to rot on the branches. The tree will ultimately end up looking untidy and unattractive.

Controlling growth

➡ My apple tree will soon be taking over the entire garden. What can I do?

'Discovery' apples

An excessively vigorous tree can be controlled in a number of ways – although the best is to make sure that you have selected a tree on an appropriate rootstock (see page 89). Rake the soil around the tree level in spring and sow grass seed. Use fine grasses, because coarse ones tend to restrict growth too much. Other methods are root-pruning (see page 94), bark-ringing (see below) and summer pruning.

The summer pruning of apple and pear trees grown as bushes is not essential (unlike trained forms, such as cordons, espaliers and fans, for which it is a vital part of their training). However, it encourages the development of high-quality fruit and checks excessive growth. Cut back lateral shoots when their bases become woody, sometime in late summer, to about 13cm (5in) from their bases. If shoots are growing from the sideshoots, trim them to just above one leaf from their bases. Do not prune the leading shoot on each branch; it will be pruned later in winter. As well as improving the quality of the fruit, removing all this growth enables light and air to enter the tree to ripen the shoots and buds. It also helps to improve the colour of the fruit.

➡ I have an apple tree that is vigorous but bears little fruit. Will bark-ringing it help?

Bark-ringing is a technique used to slow down the growth of a vigorous apple tree. The underlying principle is that removing a narrow section of bark in late spring deters the production of vegetative growth but encourages

Bark-ringing

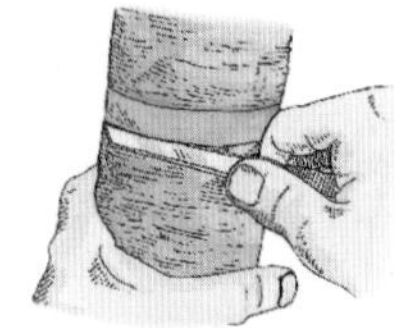

1

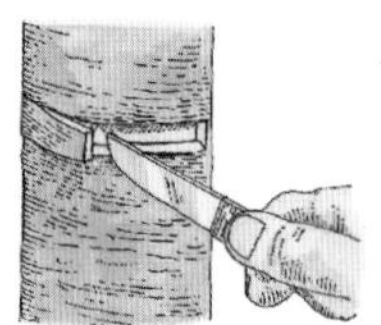

2

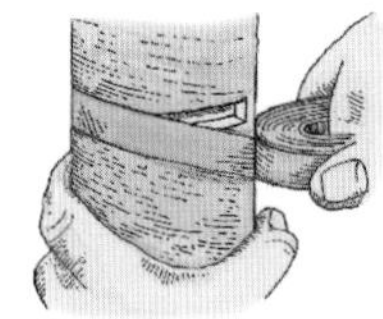

3

1 Use a sharp knife to cut just under the bark. Make two parallel cuts about 15cm (6in) below the lowest branch, no more than 6–10mm (¼–⅜in) apart..

2 Remove the bark between the two cuts, making sure that the cut area is not widened. If it is too wide, there is a chance that the tree will be killed; if it is too narrow, it is ineffective.

3 Do not paint the wound, but instead, wind several layers of adhesive tape over the cut area. Once a callus has formed over the cut, the tape can be removed; this is usually by the latter part of mid-summer.

the development of fruit. A circle of bark is cut away right down to the hardwood. Put a piece of adhesive tape around the trunk as a cutting guide and score two parallel lines right through to the hardwood beneath the bark. The width can be critical: the two cuts should be no more than 6mm (¼in) apart on a small tree and 10mm (about ⅜in) on a large one. Carefully remove the bark, taking great care not to tear it and leave snags, cover the wound with waterproof adhesive tape, which should be left in position until the wound heals. The tape should not be pushed into the cavity but just touch the outer bark on either side of the cut. This is not a technique to use unless it is really necessary, and it is appropriate only for apple trees.

The branches of my old apple tree look as if they will break under the weight of the fruit. Is there anything I can do to help?

During a tree's life, branches are bent downwards by the weight of the fruit they bear, and it is important to make sure that every branch has at least one shoot, further back from the tip, that can be used to replace the end that is bent down and to prevent it from trailing in the ground. During regular winter pruning, identify a suitable replacement shoot, which will be growing upwards on the upperside of a branch, and make sure that you do not prune it out. If the tip of the branch is weighed down, cut it back to this replacement shoot, which will in its turn, eventually, also need to be replaced.

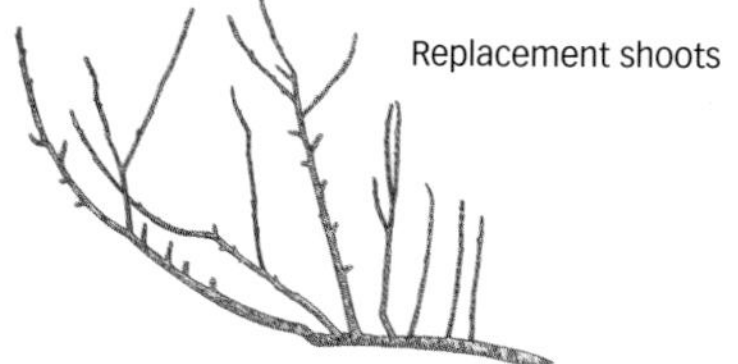

I have heard of a technique called nicking and notching. What does it mean?

This is a specialist technique used to retard a bud from growing or to promote its growth. It is used particularly when a tree's framework is being established and you may want to prevent more branches from forming or encourage an extra branch to develop. The basic idea is to make a nick just below a bud to retard it, or a similar nick, usually called a notch, above it to encourage it. The nick or notch is simply made with two cuts with a sharp knife just through the bark to the hardwood to remove a small wedge shape. The best time to do it is in spring.

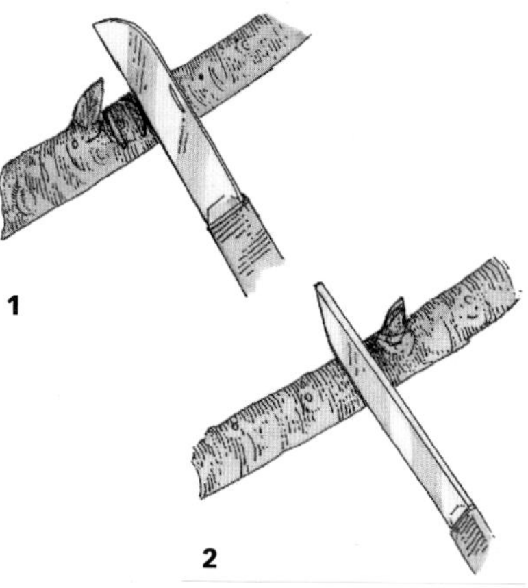

1 Notching involves using a sharp knife to make a horizontal cut, about 3mm (⅛in) deep and 6mm (¼in) above the bud. Cut out a wedge shape by slicing towards it at a 45-degree angle. Carefully remove the wedge of wood.

2 Nicking is also done with a sharp knife. Make a 3mm (⅛in) deep cut 6mm (¼in) below the bud. Make a further cut, at a 45-degree angle, so that a wedge of wood can be removed. With both notching and nicking, take care that you do not damage the bud.

Apple cordons

Cordons

➡ I do not have much space in my garden and have heard that cordons would be ideal. What do I do?

A cordon is basically a single-stemmed tree. It is tilted at an angle and its height is restricted to about 2m (6–7ft). The tree is trained up a cane, which is secured to wires. These wires are fastened horizontally between posts set 2–3m (6–10ft) apart. Alternatively, they can be fixed to a wall, preferably 10–15cm (4–6in) away from the brickwork. The lowest wire is about 75cm (30in) from the ground and the other two should be set at 60cm (2ft) intervals above this. A feathered maiden (see page 90) is planted at a 45-degree angle at some time between late autumn and early spring. It is tied to a cane that is supported at a similar angle against the wires. Cut back any sideshoots to three or four buds. Do not cut the leader. During the latter part of the following summer, once the shoots have hardened, cut them back to about three leaves. Any sideshoots that have appeared on these main shoots should be cut back to one leaf. From the next winter onwards, cut back any growth beyond the last bud. Do not allow the spurs to become overcrowded: remove any surplus. Any new shoots growing towards the top of the trunk are cut back to three or four buds. During the following summer, again cut back any hardened wood to three leaves and any sideshoots on these to one leaf. Continue with this winter and summer regime until the leader reaches just above the top wire, when it is cut back to the top of the previous year's growth. Continue with winter and summer pruning as before, but now also cut back the leader each summer to one leaf.

➡ Of all the possible methods of pruning and training apples, which would be the best to choose for a small garden?

Cordons would undoubtedly be the most suitable choice, because the trees are not only productive but you can also have several different types in a small space. If you grow several cultivars as cordons on wires, they will make an effective screen or fence within the garden, perhaps separating the ornamental and vegetable gardens. You could even arrange the wires in a circle to make an enclosed secret garden. There are some cultivars that take up hardly any space, and one or two have been specially bred so that they can be grown as 'poles'. These are, in effect, cordons and are pruned in the same way as cordons, but they are grown in containers. The main drawbacks are that the choice of cultivar is limited and, like all container-grown plants, they will need to be watered at least once every day.

How different is a multiple cordon?

A multiple cordon works in a similar way, except that two or three main stems are allowed to grow parallel with each other rather than just one. For a double cordon, the leader is cut out just above a pair of strong sideshoots and these are trained as the main stems, first along canes at a shallow angle and then vertically. In a triple cordon, the leader is also allowed to grow to form the central stem. Although single cordons are usually grown at an angle, multiple cordons are often grown vertically, but these do not produce as much fruit as those that are angled.

Pruning cordons

1 Plant a maiden tree in the dormant season and insert a strong cane slightly under the 45-degree stem. Tie the cane to the supporting wires, then the stem to the cane. Do not prune the leading shoot, but cut back lateral shoots to within three or four buds of the bases. Do not prune laterals that are shorter than this.

2 Do not let cordons bear fruit in their first growing season. Remove the blossom but take care not to damage the growth bud just behind it. In summer, cut back young shoots that develop from the cut-back laterals to one leaf beyond the base cluster. Cut back all shoots growing directly from the main stem to three or four buds.

3 In late summer of the same year, just before the leaf-fall, cut back further growth that has grown from shoots pruned back earlier. In late spring of the next year, cut back the leading shoot when it has passed the top wire.

4 When the cordon is established, in summer each year, cut back the leading shoot to leave 2–3cm (1in) of new growth. Prune back all mature lateral shoots that are growing from the main stem and are longer than 23cm (9in) to three leaves from their points of origin. Cut back shoots that are growing from existing spurs and sideshoots to one leaf beyond the rosette of leaves at their base.

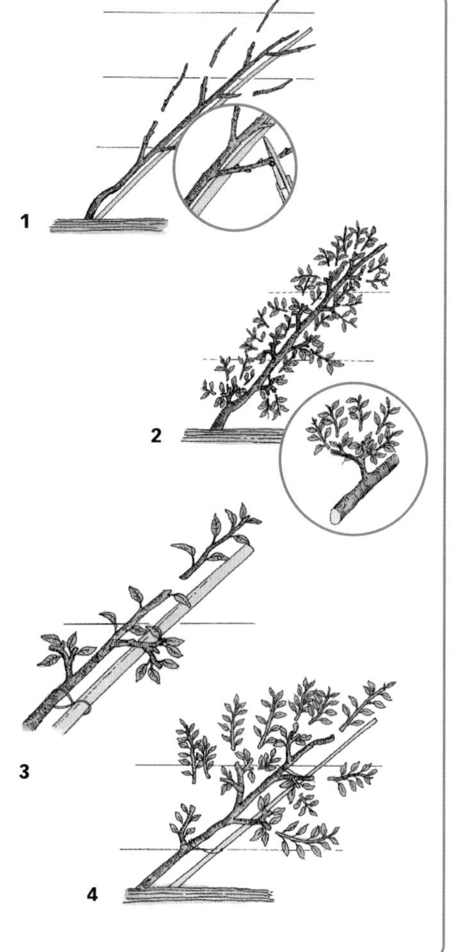

Espaliers

➡ What is an espalier and how should I prune it?

Pear tree grown as an espalier

An espalier is formed when an apple or pear tree is trained flat against a wall or wires, with one main vertical stem from which emerge a series of horizontal branches. The wires are fixed to a wall or to posts set 2–3m (6–10ft) apart. If they are against the wall, they should be held at least 10cm (4in) away from it. The two or three wires should be 40cm (16in) apart.

Uneven growth

If in summer one side of a tier is growing faster than the other, lower it slightly. Conversely, if it is much smaller than its twin, raise it. Once the tiers are formed and their ends have been cut back to fit the allotted space, prune them in the same way as for cordons (see pages 100–101).

Pruning espaliers

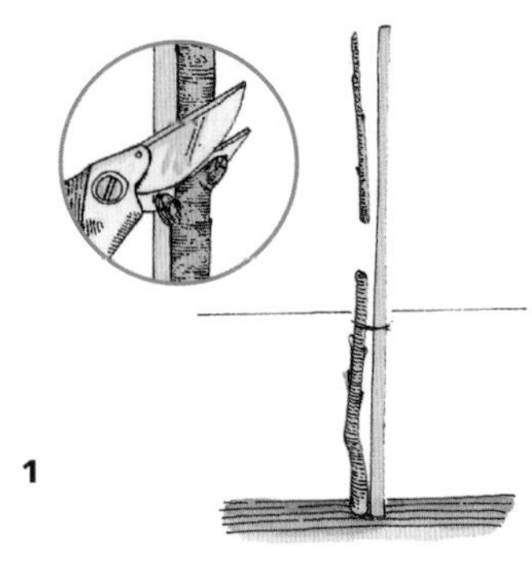

Rootstocks

Suitable rootstocks for espalier-trained apples are M27, M9, M26 and MM106; for pears choose Quince A or C.

Between late autumn and early spring, when the weather is suitable, plant a maiden whip (see page 90). Cut back the leader above the lowest wire to a bud, so that there is a pair of strong buds just below the wire. In the first summer, tie in the new leader to a vertical cane and the two sideshoots that have developed from the bud beneath the wire to canes set at 45 degrees. Any shoots lower down the stem should be cut back to two or three leaves.

At the end of the growing season, untie the canes and gently lower them so that they are horizontal. Tie the two branches to the wires. At the same time, cut back these branches by about one-third to a downward-facing bud. Cut the leader back again, this time to a bud above the second wire. Remove any sideshoots below the bottom branches completely.

During the next summer, repeat the pruning you did the previous summer by tying in the two new branches at 45 degrees. Cut back any

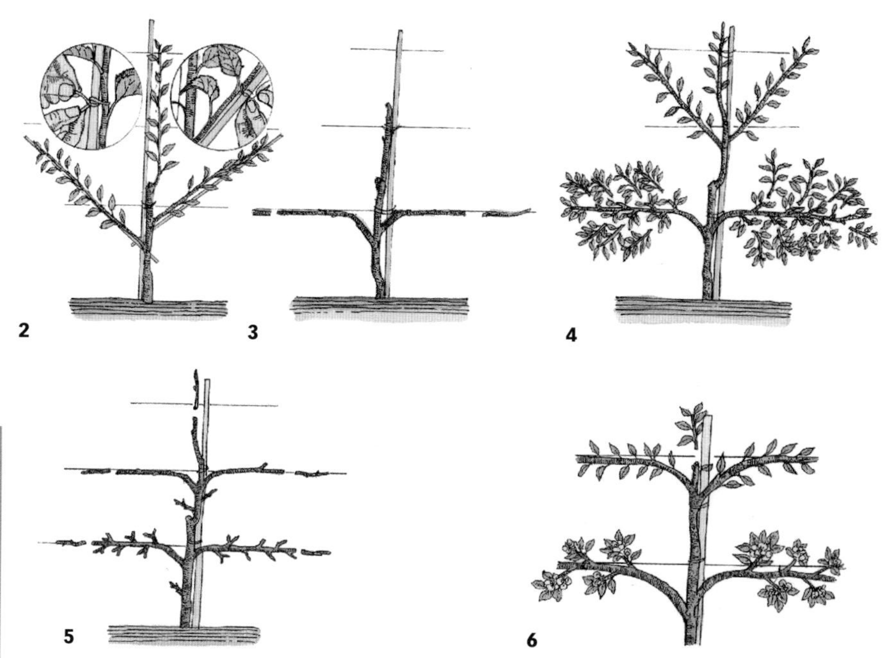

1 Plant a maiden apple or pear tree in winter. Cut back the stem to a healthy bud just above the bottom wire. There should also be two other healthy buds positioned immediately below it.

2 The top three buds will grow from early to late summer. Loosely but firmly tie the leading shoot to a vertical cane, and the two sideshoots to two others at angles of 45 degrees to the leader. Tie the canes to the wires.

3 In the following winter, cut off the leading shoot just above the next wire. Shoots will develop to form the next tier. Lower the two side branches and shorten them by a third to a healthy, strong, downward-pointing bud.

4 In summer, secure the leading and two top sideshoots to canes. Cut off any shoots growing between the first and second tier to three leaves long. Prune sideshoots on the bottom tier to three or four leaves long.

5 In subsequent winters, form further tiers in the same way as detailed earlier. Lower the tier created in summer and cut it back by one-third. Also, tip back the shoots on the lower tier.

6 In early summer, when the top wire is reached, cut off the leading shoot. When the arms fill the wires, cut off their ends. Cut back sideshoots to three leaves and sub-laterals to one leaf.

other sideshoots to three leaves and any sideshoots on the main branches to three or four leaves. Once again, in winter at the end of the growing season, lower the new branches and repeat both winter and summer pruning until the top wire has been reached. At this point, cut back the leader's new growth in winter to just one bud. In summer, cut back all new growth to three leaves above the basal cluster.

Fan-trained apple tree

Fans and step-overs

➡ Fan-trained trees always look attractive. How do I train those?

A fan is a decorative way of training a fruit tree flat against a wall or fence or against wires. The branches radiate from a short leg and are, in effect, a series of single cordons.

The horizontal wires should be set about 15cm (6in) apart, with the lowest one about 40cm (16in) above ground level. Plant a feathered maiden in winter and select two sideshoots to be the main branches. These are tied to canes, which in turn are tied to the wires at angles of about 40 degrees. Cut both shoots back to about 30cm (12in). Cut back the leader immediately above these shoots. Any other sideshoots below these should be reduced to one bud.

In the following summer, choose four or five strong shoots that appear from each of these main sideshoots and train them onto canes radiating below and above the original sideshoot. Do not fill the centre of the fan yet. Prune back any sideshoots that develop on these to about 10cm (4in). In winter, cut back the new growth of the leaders of all these main shoots to about 45cm (18in).

In the following summer (which will be the fan's second), select suitable shoots from each of the main shoots and tie them in, filling the gaps, so that it appears as a giant fan with many stems. Cut back any other sideshoots to 10cm (4in). From now on, spur-prune the fan (see pages 95–7).

Cut out old, diseased or non-productive shoots, and replace them with a suitable shoot that is allowed to develop. Canes are usually left in position. See also pages 116–17.

What is a step-over?

Apple tree trained as a step-over

A step-over is a wonderful way to use an apple tree to line a path, especially in a vegetable garden. Step-overs are most often seen in old walled gardens, but there is no reason why the method should not be used in any type of garden, as they make a perfect hedge for a small garden.

Basically, a step-over is an espalier in which only the lowest tier is used. A wire is stretched between posts about 30cm (12in) above ground. Apple trees are planted along its length at intervals of about 6m (20ft). This allows each arm of a step-over eventually to grow to about 3m (10ft) long. Once the tree becomes mature, the wire frame can be dispensed with, as the tree will hold its shape. Pruning each year, both in the formative and mature stages, is as for an espalier (see pages 102–3).

I have seen a tunnel of apples. How do I create one of these?

A walkway or pergola of apples can be a delightful feature in a garden. It can be as short as a simple archway or it can extend along a path to create an attractive, shady walk. Pears can also be grown in this way, or you could also plant a combination of apples and pears.

To start you will need a framework made of metal. You need to make sure that this framework is wide enough to allow a good path through it, plus room for the width of the trees: at least 2m (6–7ft) wide, preferably more. It should have a curved top, at least 2.1m (7ft) high, preferably 2.4m (8ft). The apple trees are planted along the sides on the outside of the framework and treated as espaliers (see pages 102–3); alternatively, they could be grown as single or multiple cordons (see pages 100–101).

Thinning apples and pears

Thinning fruit produces a better-quality crop. In early summer, bend and snap off badly formed fruits, leaving the stalks behind. Later, in midsummer, use sharp scissors or pointed secateurs to thin dessert apples, leaving one or two in each cluster spaced 10–15cm (4–6in) apart. Cooking apples should be spaced 15–20cm (6–8in) apart. Pears need less thinning; leave two fruits in each cluster.

'Vranja Nenadovic' quinces

Quinces and medlars

Are quinces easy to prune?

Yes, they are; in fact, they are much easier than most fruit trees. Quinces (*Cydonia oblonga*) can be grown either as trees with a single trunk or as multi-stemmed trees. The form with a single trunk is usually trained in the same way as for a bush apple tree with an open centre (see pages 90–91). If the plant you buy has several main stems, select the strongest and remove the others.

If you want to grow your quince as a multi-stemmed bush, it is a matter of selecting the strongest main stems and sideshoots to build a basic framework. Cut out any crossing or crowded stems. Once the tree is mature, there is virtually no pruning except to remove misplaced shoots and any dead, diseased or damaged wood.

Quince cultivars

Quinces are not widely available but are worth searching out. The two most popular cultivars are 'Meech's Prolific' and 'Vranja Nenadovic', but you could also look out for 'Champion', 'Portugal' and 'Isfahan'. Unnamed plants are also sometimes offered for sale. The fruit should be left on the tree for as long as possible, then harvested in late autumn, just before the first frosts arrive.

➡ I have bought a medlar tree. How do I prune it?

In a small garden the best way is to treat a medlar (*Mespilus germanica*) in the same way as you would a bush apple (see pages 90–91).

Plant the new tree in winter as a feathered maiden and cut back the leader to about 75cm (30in) from the ground. Cut it back to a strong sideshoot. Choose three strong, well-spaced laterals and remove the rest. Cut the remaining three back to about one-third of their original length to a strong, upward-facing bud. In the following winter, remove completely any growth that is crossing the centre of the bush. Choose a few strong growths that are suitable for continuing the development of the branch framework and reduce these by about half. Cut back any other shoots to three or four buds. Repeat this in the following winter, by which time the shape of the bush should be firmly established. From now on, it is matter of spur-pruning (see pages 95–7) to promote good fruiting as well as keeping the bush compact. Larger standard or half-standards should be trained as for apples, but thereafter need little pruning other than the usual removal of misplaced wood along with any dead, diseased or damaged wood.

➡ My quince tree throws up a number of shoots from the surrounding soil. Should I leave these?

These are suckers that are coming up from the roots. They can be left but the tree will become a thicket, reducing cropping and making it difficult to pick the fruit. Suckers are best removed as soon as they emerge. They should not be cut off above the ground level, but traced back and removed from the source by hand.

Medlars

'Merton Gage' greengages

Plums, gages and damsons: basic techniques

➡ Are plum trees pruned in the same way as apples?

No. Once established, plums and gages (*Prunus domestica*) grown as bushes, pyramids and half-standards require little pruning, although dead, crossing and rubbing branches should be removed every spring. Plums and gages are not suitable for growing as espaliers and cordons, although they are often cultivated as fan-trained trees against a warm wall.

The other fundamental difference is that plums can suffer from a disease called silverleaf (see pages 149–50), and any necessary pruning is carried out in summer rather than winter. Once trees are established, all they really need is to have any dead or damaged wood removed. Although most gardeners no longer paint the wounds on trees (see page 151), many make an exception for plums and paint any wounds with a bituminous compound, which is available from most garden centres.

➡ How do I train a plum tree?

The best type of plum tree is a half-standard. In early spring, plant a feathered maiden on the appropriate stock and stake it firmly. Select three or four strong sideshoots, the lowest one about 1.2m (4ft) from the ground. Prune these back by up to half their length to a good bud. Remove all other sideshoots. Cut back the leader just above the top sideshoot.

In the following early spring, select three or four sideshoots on each of the branches and reduce these to about half, removing all other

Feathered maiden 'Victoria' plum tree

Pruning a bush plum

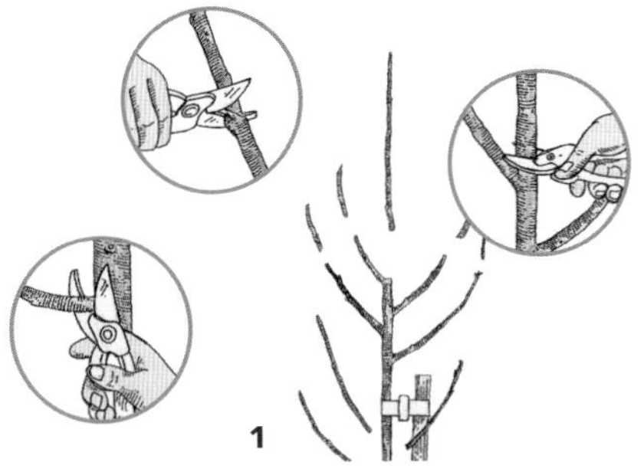

1 Begin by establishing an open framework of outward-facing branches.

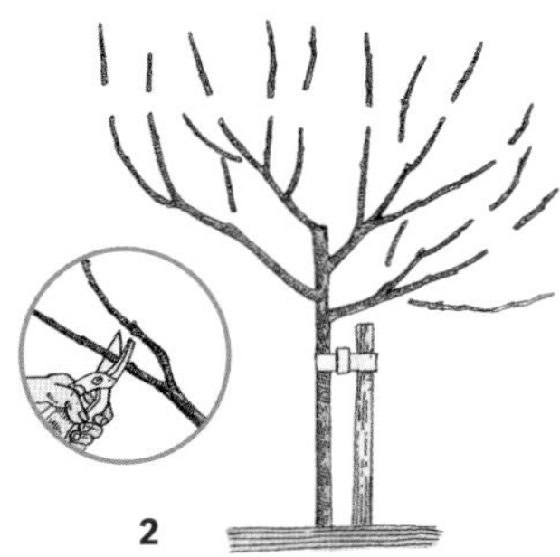

2 In subsequent years, cut shoots back out inward-facing shoots.

shoots. From now on, prune only in summer. It is only necessary to take out any dead, diseased or damaged wood along with any shoots that cross back through the centre of the tree or that rub against other branches.

How do I train a bush plum tree?

Begin by planting a two-year-old (feathered maiden) tree in late autumn or early winter. Do not plant it in late winter as growth often begins early in spring. Start pruning a bush plum in late winter or early spring when growth begins and the buds start to break. Cut the central stem about 1m (3ft) above the ground and slightly above a sideshoot. There should be three strong shoots below it. Prune each of these main shoots back by half to two-thirds, severing them just above an outward-facing bud. Then cut off, flush with the main stem, all sideshoots below the top four shoots.

In early spring of the following year, prune the bush, which will be three years old. The lateral shoots that were pruned back in the previous year will have produced extension growths. Prune these back by about half. At the same time, cut out at their bases all other shoots growing from the main shoots. At this stage, the bush will have about eight, well-spaced and strong stems. In the following years, little pruning is needed, other than cutting out dead or crossing branches in summer. Remove suckers from the ground and cut off shoots that are growing from the trunk below the lowest main branch. Regularly check that the bush is securely staked.

Half-standard plum trees

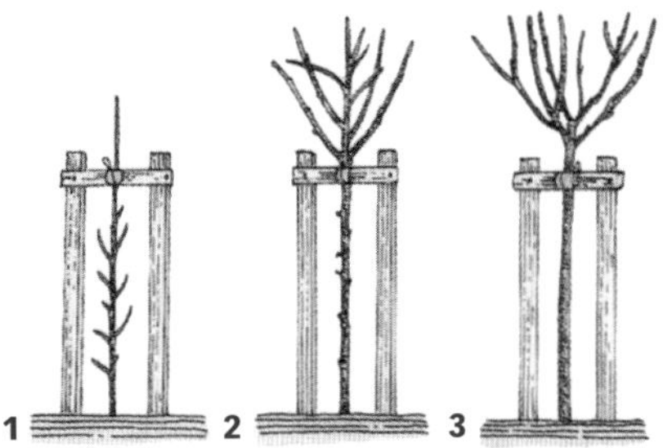

1 In early spring, plant a feathered maiden and make sure it is firmly staked.

2 Remove any sideshoots on the lower part of the main stem.

3 Shorten the main sideshoots by about half.

What is a pyramid plum tree?

Pyramid plum trees are a way of producing a tree-shaped plum tree without having to grow a large tree. They are small enough for small and medium gardens. If it is grown on Pixy stock (see below) it will grow to about 2m (about 6ft), and on St Julien A to about 2.4m (8ft). Plant a feathered maiden in winter and stake it well. Reduce the leader to a strong bud about 1.5m (5ft) above the ground. Cut back all the sideshoots above about 45cm (18in) to about half their length and remove any below this height. In the tree's first summer, prune back all the new growth on these and any new main sideshoots by about half to a downward-facing bud. Any sideshoots that have grown on these main shoots should be cut back to about 15cm (6in).

In early spring, cut back the new growth on the leader by about two-thirds. Repeat the summer pruning until the tree has reached its required height and shape, when the new growth on the leader should be cut back to one bud in the early spring. Continue to summer prune, removing any vigorous, upward-pointing or crossing wood, along with any dead, dying or damaged wood.

Pruning a pyramid tree

1 Plant a feathered maiden and make sure it is securely staked.

'Prince Englebert' plums

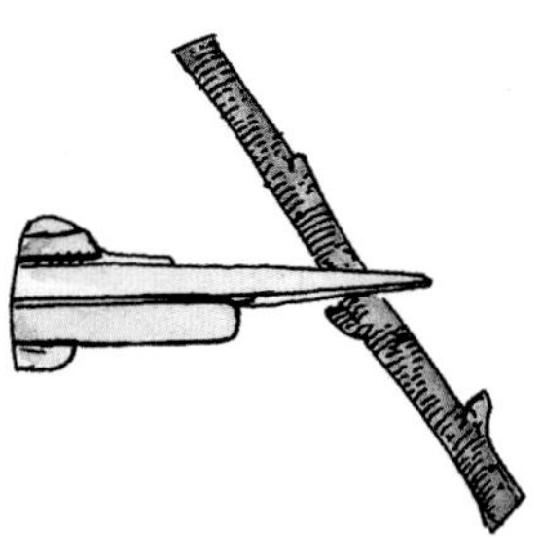

2 Cut back the leader to about 1.5m (5ft) above the ground.

3 Shorten sideshoots to about half their length.

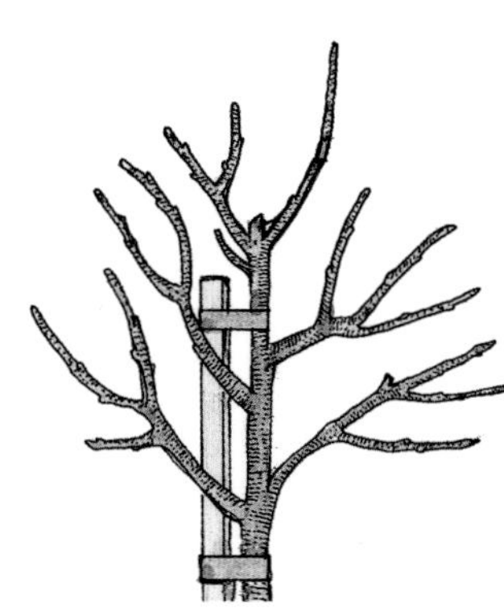

4 Prune new growth in early spring.

5 In summer shorten the current season's growth.

Rootstocks for plums, gages and damsons

Trees grown on rootstocks marked with an asterisk (*) are suitable for small and medium-sized gardens.

Pixy*	Dwarfing stock	Bush, pyramid, spindle bush
St Julien A*	Semi-vigorous stock	Bush, fan, pyramid, spindle bush
Brompton A	Vigorous stock	Half-standard, standard
Myrobalan B	Vigorous stock	Half-standard, standard

'Bradley's King' damsons

Established trees

➡ There is an old damson tree in my garden. What do I do with it?

Damsons (*Prunus insititia*) are a form of plum and are treated in the same way, except that they generally receive even less attention. Many damson trees are grown in hedgerows or beside farm tracks and are never pruned from one year to the next; yet they still seem to produce an ample supply of fruit. You will improve cropping by removing all damaged, diseased and misplaced branches in summer, cutting back to healthy wood. Otherwise, you need do nothing.

➡ I have an old plum tree, which has never been pruned and is overcrowded. What should I do to it?

If the tree is not rotten or too damaged, it can be rescued with a bit of careful pruning. The method is the same as for a neglected apple tree (see pages 146–7), except the work should be carried out in summer rather than winter to avoid silverleaf becoming a problem. The other difference is that, although it is now not usual practice to paint wounds on trees, any large wounds on a plum tree should be covered with a bituminous paint (available from garden centres) to protect the tree against infection.

➡ I know that plum fans take up a lot of space but I would like to try to grow one. How do I do it?

The branches should radiate from a short leg, producing an ever-increasing number of ribs. They are attached to canes, which are fastened to wires. The horizontal wires should be set about 15cm (6in) apart, with the lowest about 40cm (16in) above ground. Plant a feathered maiden in winter and select two sideshoots as the main branches. These are tied to canes, which are tied to the wires at angles of about 45 degrees, and each shoot is cut back to about

Damson cultivars

The following damson cultivars are reliable:

- Early: 'Merryweather'
- Mid-season: 'Bradley's King' and 'Farleigh'
- Late: 'Frogmore Damson' and 'Prune'

30cm (12in). The leader is cut off immediately above these shoots. Any other sideshoots below these are reduced to one bud. In the following summer, choose four or five strong shoots that appear from each of these main sideshoots and train them on to canes radiating below and above the original sideshoot, but do not fill the centre of the fan yet. Prune back any sideshoots that develop on these to about 10cm (4in) in length.

In early spring, cut back the new growth of the leaders of all these main shoots to about 45cm (18in). During the following summer (the fan's second), select suitable shoots from each of the main shoots and tie these in, filling the gaps, so that it looks like a giant fan with many stems. Again, cut back any other sideshoots to 10cm (4in).

Once the shape of the fan has become established, prune in early spring every year by removing any shoots that grow either towards the wall or away from it as well as any that are overcrowding the basic fan, so that all new sideshoots are at least 10cm (4in) apart. Any remaining shoots should be cut back to three leaves after fruiting. If shoots become old, diseased or non-productive, cut them out and replace them with a suitable replacement shoot that is allowed to develop (see page 99). The canes will have to be left in position.

My 'Victoria' plum has many bare shoots with no buds. What have I done wrong?

It is most likely that the failure to crop is nothing to do with your pruning: it is more probable that the culprits are bullfinches. These birds spend winter in twos or more eating the buds of certain trees, and plum trees are among their favourites. If the trees are small, they can be netted to keep the birds out and the tree should blossom. If you do not use a net, check the trees in early spring, and if the shoots have been stripped cut them back to a strong bud to promote growth to replace the damaged shoots.

'Victoria' plums

Are gages treated in the same way as plums?

Yes, gages are a type of plum, and as far as rootstocks, types of tree and pruning are concerned, they are treated in exactly the same way as plums.

I have recently seen some bullace trees for sale. How would I cope with one?

Bullaces are a type of small plum, and they may be black, blue, yellow or white. They make neat trees, 3–6m (10–20ft) high and across. They are often grown in hedgerows in a similar manner to damsons, and are usually pruned in the same way – that is, they are simply neglected, except for the removal of dead and diseased wood.

Peaches and nectarines

'Peregrine' peaches

How should I train a peach tree?

Peaches (*Prunus persica*) are normally grown as either bushes or fans, as are nectarines (*P. persica* var. *nectarina*). Fans are in many ways the best method, especially because they are easier to protect against frost and attack by birds. Like sour cherries, peaches fruit on wood produced during the previous year, so the key is to use renewal pruning to ensure a continuous supply of new shoots.

The basic peach or nectarien fan is trained in the normal way; see Pruning a fan-trained fruit tree (pages 116–17).

Peach fans take up a lot of wall space. Can I produce a bush instead?

Peaches produce fruit on the previous year's growth, and the aim is to produce an open-centred bush, which is pruned by a renewal process. Plant a feathered maiden in winter or early spring. Prune back the leader to a good sideshoot about 75cm (30in) above the ground. Select three or four main sideshoots below this cut and reduce them all by about two-thirds. Remove all other shoots. In the following year in early spring, cut back all the shoots you need to make a basic framework by about half. Reduce

Rootstocks for peaches and nectarines

St Julien A	Semi-vigorous	Bush, fan
Brompton A	Vigorous	Bush
Seedling peach	Vigorous	Bush

the remaining sideshoots on the main branches to about 10cm (4in). The framework is then established and any future pruning is simply to remove misplaced or dead wood. Cut out a few of the older fruited shoots in summer.

'Lord Napier' nectarines

Pruning a bush peach tree

1 Plant a feathered maiden in early spring, and cut back the leading shoot to a good sideshoot. Cut back three or four lateral shoots below this by two-thirds. Remove all other laterals close to the main stem.

2 In the subsequent year, cut back by half all shoots growing from the main laterals.

3 In early spring of the following year, cut back by half the young shoots that developed from shoots that were cut back in the previous spring. Also remove any branches that cross and crowd the centre of the bush.

4 In the following year, remove old shoots, those that cross the bush's centre and those that cause congestion, thus preventing the circulation of air and entry of light.

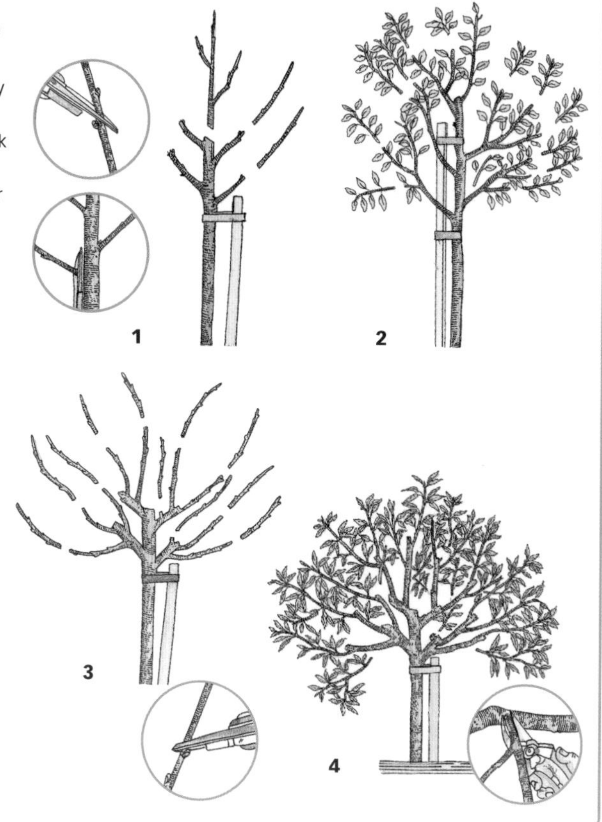

Pruning a fan-trained fruit tree

1

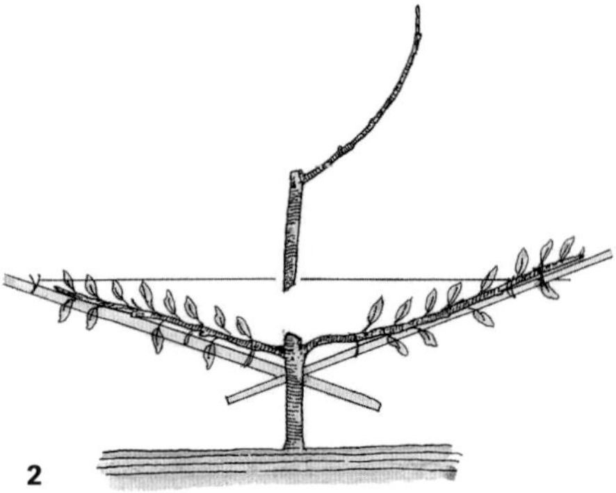

2

3

4

1 Plant a feathered maiden in winter, and in late winter cut back the main stem to about 60cm (2ft) above the ground and slightly above a strong lateral. Cut back all other laterals to one bud from their bases. In early summer, a few shoots will have formed: remove all but the top one and two others, lower down and preferably opposite each other.

2 In late summer, cut back the central stem and tie each of the two arms to individual canes, which are tied to the supporting wires. Cut back the leader of each arm.

3 In early spring, cut back the two arms to a bud. Cut the stems 30–45cm (12–15in) from the leader.

4 In late spring and summer, select three or four strong shoots – two on the upper side and one or two on the lower part – on each of the arms. Cut off all other sideshoots, leaving one leaf at the base of each one. For each of these six to eight shoots tie a strong cane to the tiers of wires and secure the shoot to it.

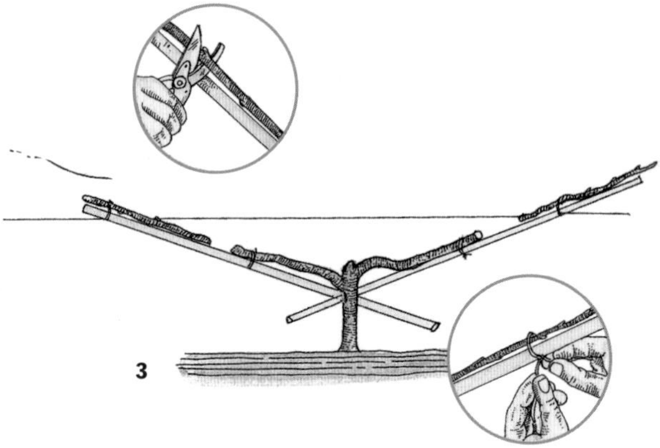

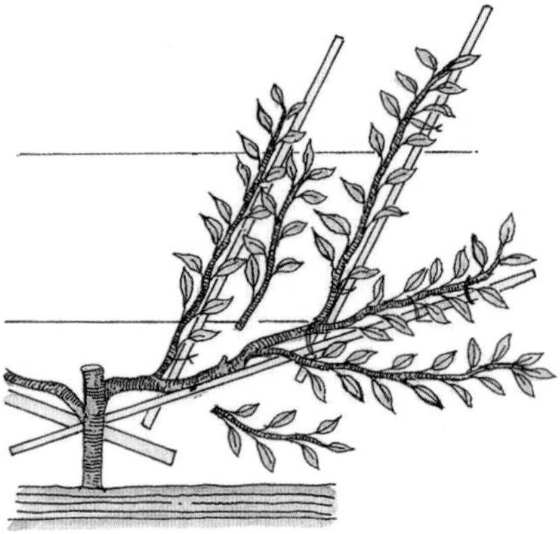

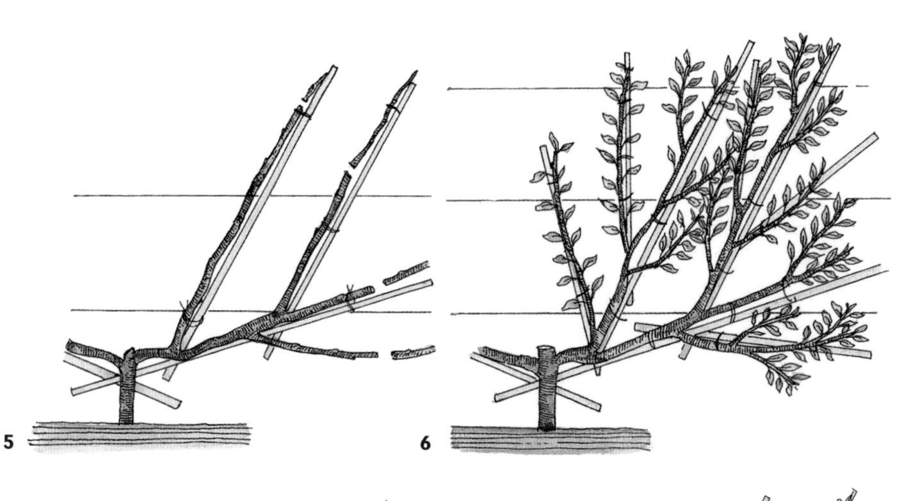

5 In early spring, cut back the new growth on each of these six to eight shoots by about one-third. Make these cuts slightly above a downward-pointing growth bud.

6 In summer, let the ends of the shoots grow naturally. Allow three new shoots to develop on each arm and tie them to canes and then to the wires. Rub out buds growing towards the wall. Allow shoots to grow every 10cm (4in) along the upper and lower sides of the ribs.

7 In late summer, cut out the growing points of the lateral shoots. These are the young shoots that will bear fruit in the following year.

8 In late spring and summer of the following year, remove shoots that are growing towards and away from the wall. If they have flowerbuds at their bases, cut them to two leaves long.

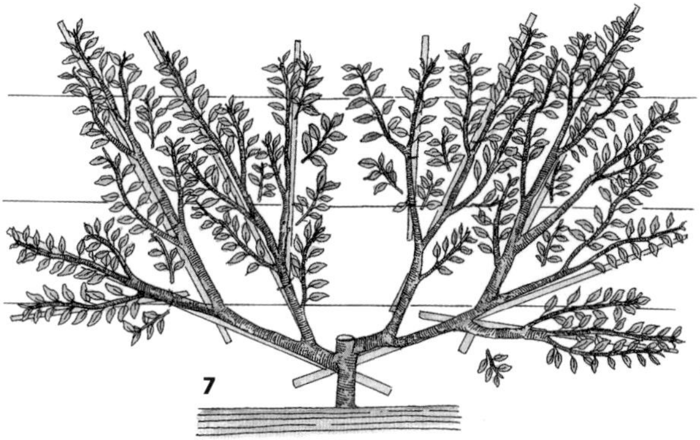

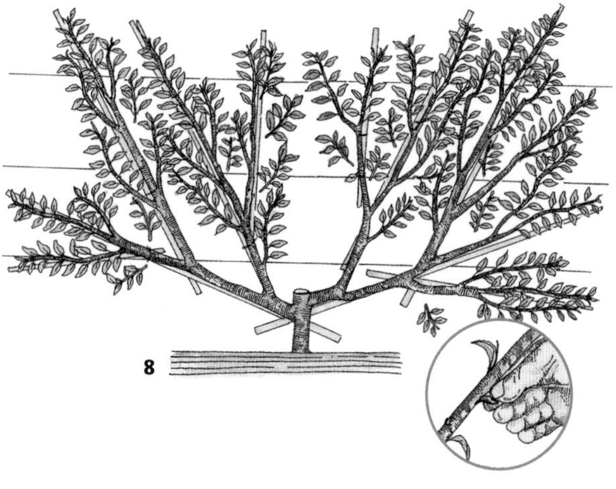

Fan-trained Morello cherry tree

Cherries

➡ Are cherries easy to grow?

There are two types of cherry: sweet cherries (*Prunus avium*) and sour cherries (*P. cerasus*). Sour or acid cherries are mainly used in cooking because they are not sweet enough to eat straight from the tree.

Cherries used to be regarded as the most unsuitable of fruit to grow in the garden because until recently they could not be grown on a dwarf stock, and the full-sized trees were too large for most gardens. In the past, acid cherries were the more popular form, but new, self-fertile sweet cherries have become more widely grown.

Rootstocks for cherries

Colt	Semi-dwarfing	Bush, fan
Malling F12/1	Vigorous	Half-standard

Growing a fan-trained sweet cherry

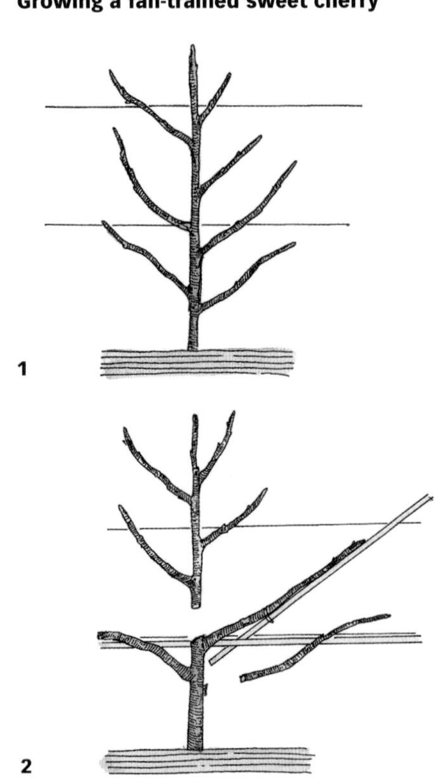

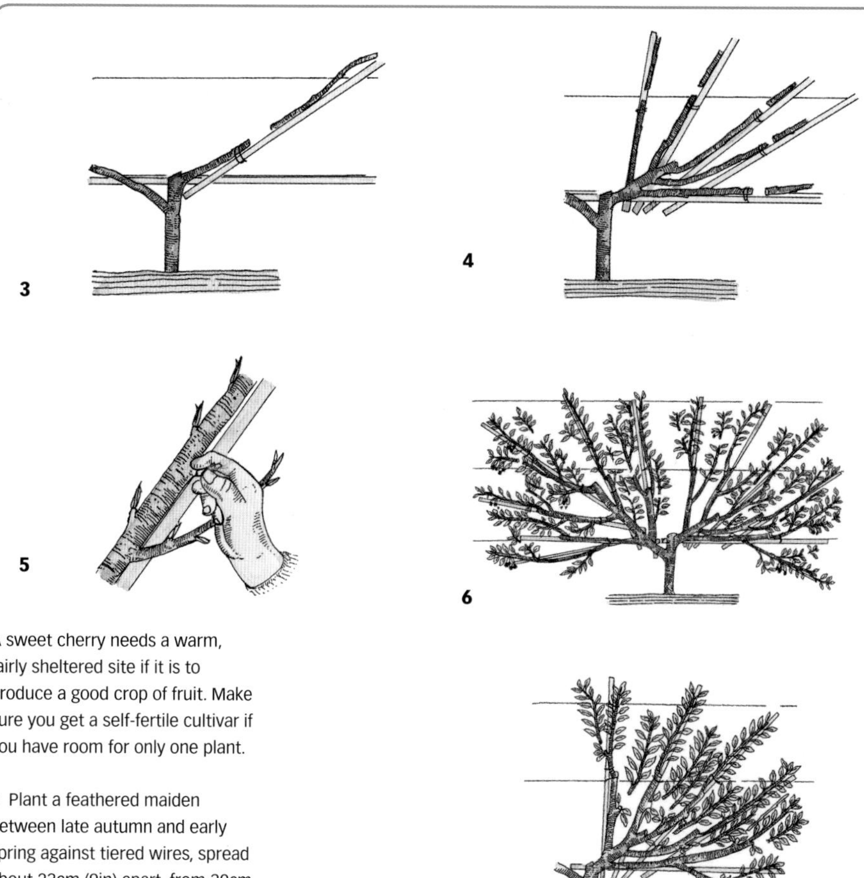

A sweet cherry needs a warm, fairly sheltered site if it is to produce a good crop of fruit. Make sure you get a self-fertile cultivar if you have room for only one plant.

1 Plant a feathered maiden between late autumn and early spring against tiered wires, spread about 23cm (9in) apart, from 30cm (12in) above the ground to about 2.1m (7ft) high.

2 In the following spring select two strong sideshoots near the base and cut off the central stem, just above the top one. Tie the sideshoots to two canes at 45 degrees, then to the wires.

3 In spring of the following year, cut each lateral shoot to about 30cm (12in) from the central stem, cutting slightly above an outward-pointing bud.

4 In summer, shoots grow from the two arms. Tie them to canes and train them into position. In the spring, cut them back to outward-pointing buds, leaving 45–50cm (18–20in) of new growth.

5 In the following spring (and annually thereafter), rub out young shoots that are growing outwards or towards the wall. Make sure that shoots are equally spaced.

6 In late summer of the same year, cut back to five or six leaves all shoots that are not needed to extend or build up the framework. Tie in sideshoots that are required to fill up bare areas or to replace old wood.

7 In early autumn, cut back to three leaves all lateral shoots that were cut back to five or six leaves in midsummer.

Sweet cherries

Cherries can be grown as bushes or, if you have the space, as half-standards, but many gardeners like to grow them as fans against a wall or fence. They not only look attractive but are easy to cover with nets to protect from birds. Fans are trained in the same way as for plums (see pages 116–17). Cherries fruit on older wood of two years or more, so spur-pruning is required (see pages 95–7). Bushes and half-standards are also treated as the equivalent plums (see page 109).

➡ Are sour cherries pruned in the same way as sweet cherries?

Not quite. They are grown on the same type of trees – fans, bushes and half-standards – but sour cherries fruit on one-year-old wood, while sweet cherries fruit on two-year-old wood. It is important, therefore, that there is a constant renewal of wood, and so, once the fan or other form has been formed, they are pruned using renewal pruning. Cut out in spring any overcrowded or misplaced shoots and reduce the remainder to about 10cm (4in) apart. Once fruiting has taken place prune the fruiting shoot back to a new shoot.

Growing a fan-trained sour cherry

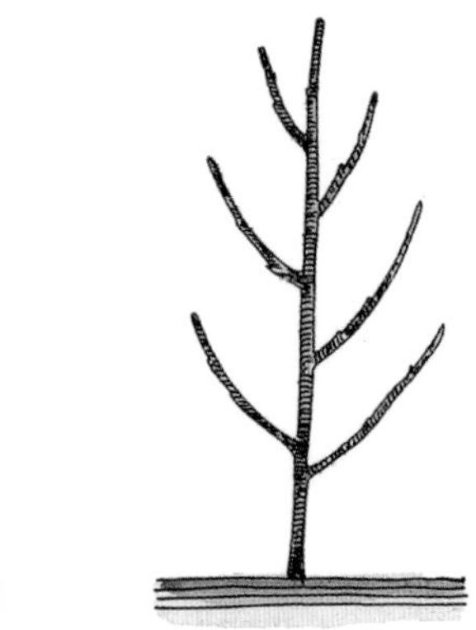

1

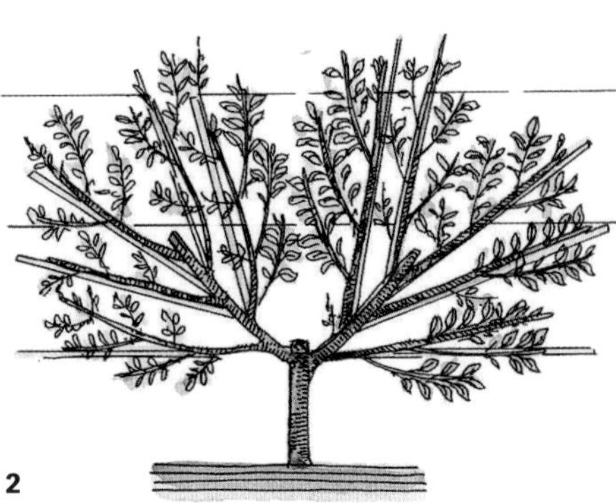

2

1 The pruning of a fan-trained sour cherry for the first three years is exactly the same as recommended for a fan-trained peach tree (see pages 116–17).

2 In the third year, allow the leading shoots on each rib to create extension growth and tie these to strong canes that are firmly secured to the wires.

3 In late spring of the fourth and subsequent years, thin out new shoots to 10–15cm (4–6in) apart and tie them to the wires while they are still flexible. Cut out at

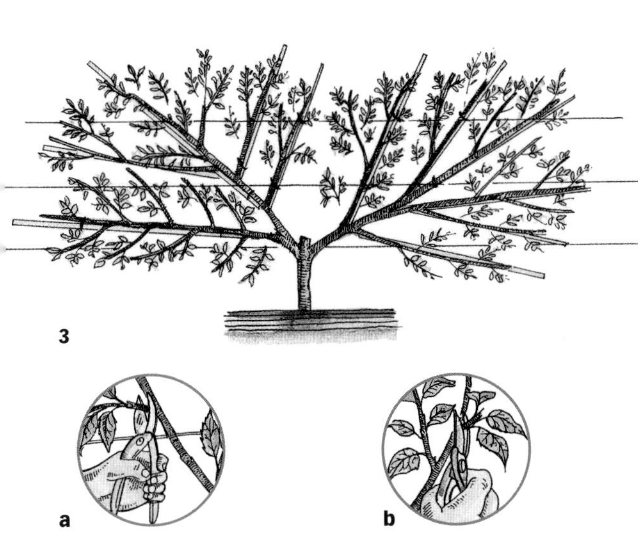

their bases all shoots that point directly at the wall (**a**). Leave a replacement shoot at the base of each lateral that will bear fruit (**b**). Where there is room allow the ends of the young shoots to grow naturally so they can clothe the wall with growth.

4 In the fourth and subsequent years, cut out lateral shoots that have borne fruit to the young replacement shoot that was left when pruning in spring (**a**). Cut out shoots that have developed in summer and are pointing either towards the wall or directly away from it (**b**). Inspect all shoots to make sure that they are tied securely to the canes and wires (**c**).

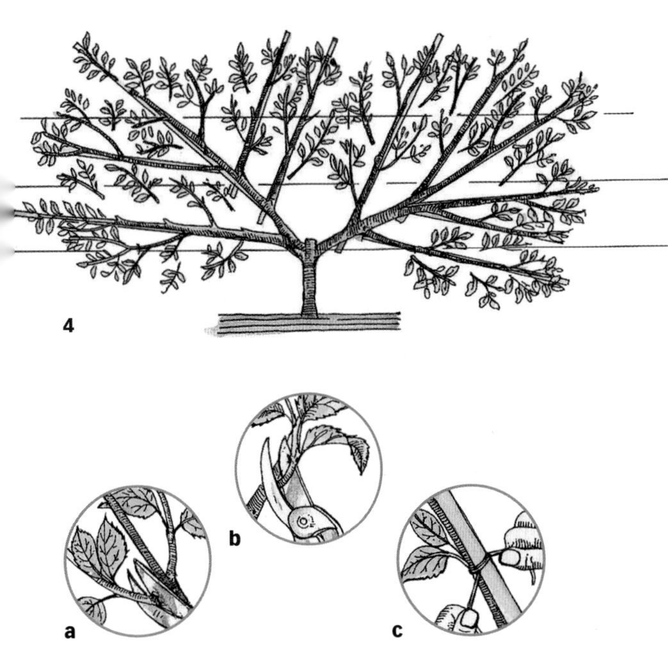

Figs, elderberries and mulberries

What is the best way to grow a fig tree?

Figs can be grown as bush trees or as fans. In cooler areas, training a fig against a wall provides it with necessary protection. The initial training of fig fans is the same as for cherries or peaches. Generally the shape is not as regular as for other fans, with more space being left between the main stems, and canes are often dispensed with (see opposite).

Once the framework is established, renewal pruning is required. In early spring, tie in some new shoots as replacements into gaps. Reduce others to one bud as the new fruiting wood. Finally, remove any others. Cut out all old fruited wood along with any dead or misplaced wood. It is important not to let the branches become too overcrowded, because as much light and warmth as possible should be allowed to reach the new growths.

I have often wondered if I could grow a mulberry tree. How should it be pruned?

Black mulberries (*Morus nigra*) are grown as trees, which may be either standards or half-standards. They can live to incredible ages, often several centuries, and require little work.

Restricting fig roots

The roots of fig trees must be constrained to prevent them from producing masses of leafy growth and few fruits. Prepare the planting area by digging a hole 60cm (2ft) square and deep. Line it with bricks or paving slabs and fill with 30cm (12in) of rubble. Then fill with soil and rubble.

In the initial stages, prune them so that they have a good framework of about five or six good branches. After that, as usual it is just a question of removing any dead or damaged branches and anything that grows so that it rubs against other branches or back into centre of the tree. The best time to prune is in winter before growth starts. If you prune later, the cut stems will bleed. Staunch the flow with a flame from a cigarette lighter, a match or even a piece of hot metal.

Can elderberries be grown in the garden?

Elderberries

Yes. Although it is the berries of the common elder (*Sambucus nigra*) that are frequently fermented to make elderberry wine, the sweet elder (*S. canadensis*) has several cultivars which provide fine black berries. Look out for 'Adams', 'Kent', 'Nova' and 'York'. After planting bare-rooted plants in winter, prune back healthy shoots to outward-facing buds. Completely cut out thin, diseased and crossing shoots. In winter, cut out some old shoots at ground level to encourage the development of new ones and also cut out dead and diseased shoots.

Fan-training a fig

1

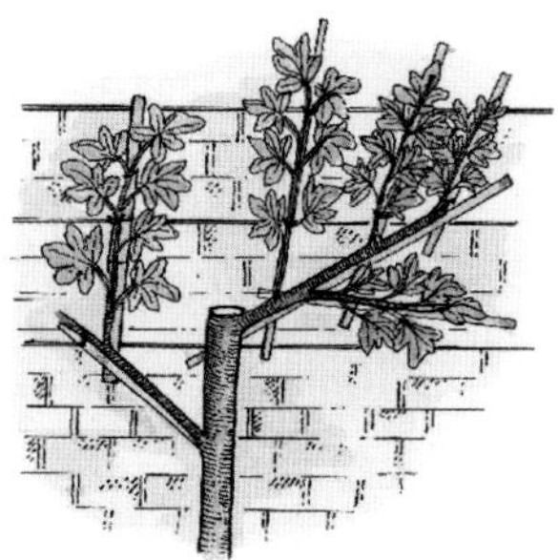
2

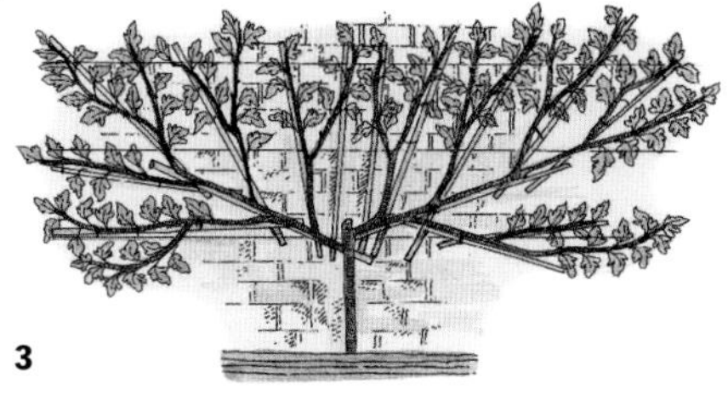
3

1 In winter, plant a two-year-old fig tree 15–20cm (6–8in) away from the base of the wall. Erect supporting wires, 23cm (9in) apart, from 45cm (18in) above the ground to the top of the wall. In spring, cut back the central stem to just above the lowest wire and immediately above a lateral shoot. Select this and another below it to form the arms and tie them to canes secured at 45 degrees to the wires. Cut back both arms to a bud 45cm (18in) from the trunk. Cut off other laterals.

2 Next summer, allow four shoots to grow from each of the two arms: one at the end of the arm to form extension growth, one from the underside and two on the top side. Rub out all other buds growing from the arms and secure the eight shoots to canes. The aim is to form a strong framework of well-spaced branches. Allow plenty of space between the newly formed ribs, because fig leaves are large and create a great deal of shade.

3 In late winter of the following year, prune back each of the main shoots, cutting slightly above a bud, which will then continue its growth in the desired direction; leave about 60cm (2ft) of the previous season's growth. In summer, allow further shoots to develop. Rub out unwanted buds.

4 It often takes four years to create a framework of evenly spaced ribs on the fan. Once this has been achieved, the routine is to prune the fan in spring and again in summer. In spring, use sharp secateurs to cut out diseased and frost-damaged shoots (**a**). Thin out young shoots to just above one bud from their base (**b**). Position and tie in young shoots (**c**). Completely remove shoots growing towards and away from the wall (**d**). Cut out some of the old, bare shoots to slightly above the first bud from its base (**e**). Later in the year, in early summer, cut back young growths to five leaves from their base.

a
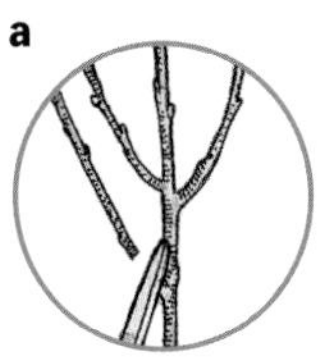
b
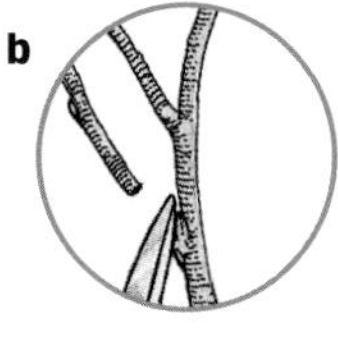
c
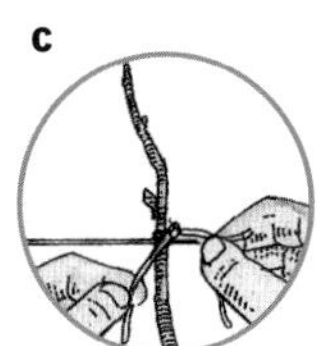
d
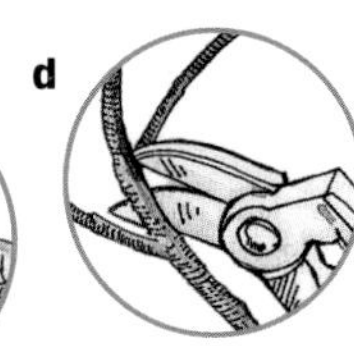
e
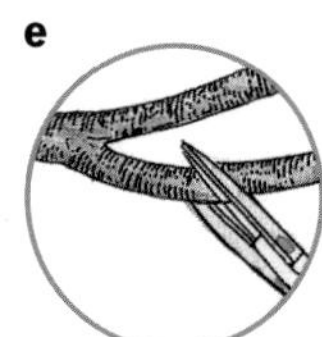

4

Almonds, walnuts and cobnuts

Are almonds difficult to prune?

Almonds (*Prunus dulcis*) are grown for their nuts rather than fleshy fruit, but they are treated in the same way as peaches are (see pages 114–15), usually being grown as bushes. Almonds produce their fruit on the previous year's growth, and so the aim is to produce an open-centred bush, which is pruned by a renewal process.

Plant a feathered maiden in winter or early spring. Prune back the leader to a good sideshoot about 75cm (30in) above the ground. Select three or four main sideshoots below this, cut and reduce them all by about two-thirds. Remove all other shoots completely. In the following year in early spring, choose all the shoots you need to make a basic framework and cut these back by about half, as usual to a strong bud. Reduce all the remaining sideshoots on the main branches to about 10cm (4in). Once the framework is established, any future pruning is to remove misplaced or dead wood.

Almond cultivars

Although they are not widely available, the following self-fertile cultivars are worth seeking out: 'Ayles', Guara' and 'Steliette'. 'Ferraduel' and 'Ferragnes' are only partly self-fertile.

Almond blossom

Walnuts

In addition, take out a few of the older fruited shoots in summer in order to promote new and refreshed growth.

I have recently planted a walnut tree in my garden. What should I do next?

Walnuts (*Juglans regia*) are simple to deal with. They are grown as a tree with a central trunk and leader. In the first one or two winters, prune in such a way as to develop a good framework of main branches, making sure that they are well spaced and do not cross. Other than that there is little to do. Keep an eye out for any misplaced branches – those that cross back into the tree or grow vertically, for example – and cut these out. Also, as usual, remove any dead or damaged wood.

Pruning should be undertaken in winter before the tree starts into growth because the cuts are inclined to bleed sap once growth has restarted.

Walnut cultivars

The following walnuts are self-fertile: 'Broadview', 'Buccaneer', 'Franquette', 'Lara', 'Mayette' and 'Parisienne'.

I have always liked cobnuts and would like to grow them. How do I prune them?

Cobnuts (*Corylus avellana*) can be left to develop many-stemmed bushes with just the older and dead material being removed, but this is an unproductive method and takes up a lot of space. A much better way is to grow a cobnut as an open-centred bush.

Plant a maiden tree in winter and cut back the leader to about 50cm (20in) above the soil. Remove any shoots that arise below about 45cm (18in) and allow any above this to develop into the basic framework. Over the next two winters, allow this to increase to up to 12 main branches. In the winter after these have developed, cut them back by about one-third. Remove any that are too vigorous, grow vertically or are misplaced.

Cobnuts are pruned in late summer by a method that is unique to the species. It is known as 'brutting'. The main sideshoots are broken, not cut, about halfway along and allowed to hang down. This encourages the development of flowerbuds for the following year. Once pollination is over in spring, cut back these shoots to three or four buds, removing the broken piece. At the same time, take out one or two of the older shoots to promote new ones.

What are filberts and how would I prune them?

Filberts (*Corylus maxima*) are similar to cobnuts and are treated in exactly the same way as far as pruning is concerned. Hazelnuts are also treated in this way.

Soft Fruit

Redcurrants and whitecurrants

➡ How do I prune redcurrants and whitecurrants?

Redcurrants (*Ribes rubrum*) are usually grown as bushes, and formative pruning starts as soon as you plant the bush, which should be in winter, during the plant's dormancy. Cut back all stems by about half to an outward-facing bud. In the following winter, cut back all leaders and outward-facing sideshoots by about half. Any inward-facing sideshoots should be cut out completely or reduced to about one bud or 2–3cm (about 1in) long. Remove any new shoots that have appeared below the main framework of branches. The aim is to create a bush with a short stem or 'leg' from which the branches develop.

By the following year, the bushes will be mature, and all that is needed is to cut back the new wood of the leaders by about half and all sideshoots to one or two buds or 2–3cm (about 1in). If you have time it can be useful to cut back the sideshoots in summer to three or four buds or about 10cm (4in). This lets in more light, which helps to ripen the fruit. Whitecurrants are the same fruit, but have pearly white skins. They are trained and pruned in exactly the same way.

Bush-grown redcurrants

1 In the first winter, prune all shoots by half, cutting them back to just above an outward-facing bud. Repeat the process in the second winter and cut outward-facing sideshoots by half.

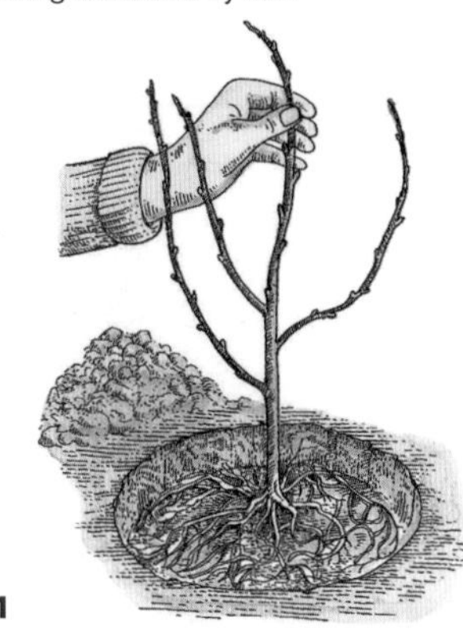

1

2 In the third winter, cut leaders back by about 15cm (6in) or half, and laterals to one or two buds from the base.

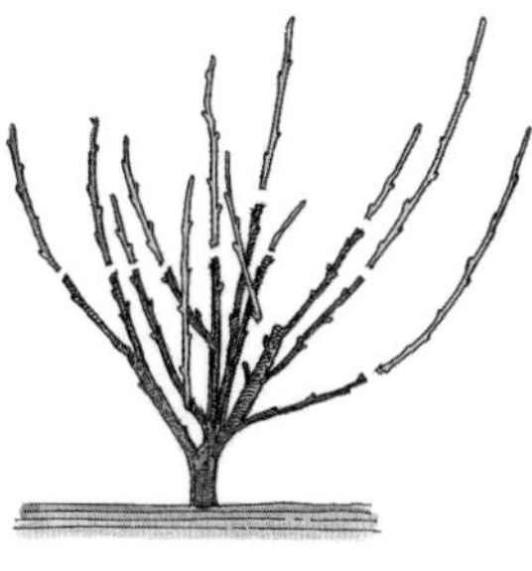

2

3 In fourth and subsequent winters, cut back leading shoots to keep plants neat.

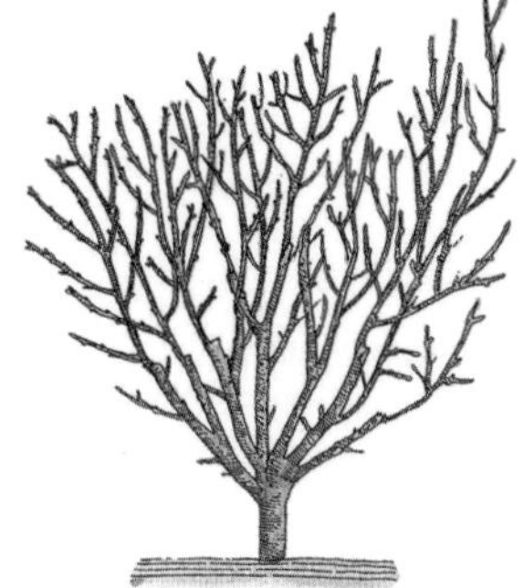

3

Are redcurrants always grown as bushes, or can I train plants in a more decorative way?

Redcurrants can be trained in several attractive ways, which makes them useful additions to a decorative potager. They can be trained as espaliers, cordons or fans. These can be against wires in a fruit cage or decoratively set against a wall.

Espaliers are trained against a set of parallel wires, set about 30cm (12in) apart and to about 1.5m (5ft) above the ground. The young plant is set against the wires and two shoots are trained sideways with a leader trained vertically against a cane. All other shoots are removed. In the second year, two new sideshoots are trained along the next wires, and so on every year until the top wire is reached by the leader. Every winter, the new growth is cut back to one bud or 2–3cm (about 1in), on both the main branches and their sideshoots.

Redcurrant fans are developed in a similar way except that the side branches are allowed to form from a short leg and are tied in to radiating canes rather than along horizontal wires.

Cordons are essentially single-stemmed bushes, and they have the advantage that they take up much less space than a bush. Once planted, the leader of the young plant is cut back by a half and all sideshoots are reduced to one bud or 2–3cm (about 1in). The leader is tied in a vertical position to a cane. The leader and sideshoots are reduced in this way every winter. Once the cordon has reached its required height, the leader is also cut back to one bud each winter. As with bush redcurrants, it can be a good idea to prune back the sideshoots to about five leaves or 10cm (4in) in summer to allow the light to get to the fruit.

Cordon redcurrants

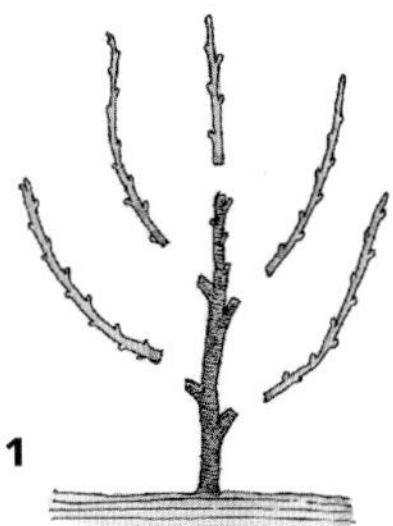

1 Plant one-year-old bushes in winter, setting them 38cm (15in) apart. Shorten the central shoot by about half its length, cutting to an outward-facing bud. Cut back lateral shoots to one bud from their base, but completely remove those within 10cm (4in) of the ground.

2 In early midsummer of the next year, prune back the current season's sideshoots to four or five leaves from their base. Do not prune the leading shoot at this stage but make sure that the new growth is tied to the supporting stake.

3 In the second and subsequent years, prune in winter. Cut back the leading shoot to just above a healthy bud and remove all but 15cm (6in) of the new growth. In later years, cut back the leading shoot to one bud of new growth and cut back to leave 2.5cm (1in) of new growth on all lateral shoots that were pruned the summer before.

4 During the following, and all subsequent summers, leave pruning the leading shoot until winter, but cut back the sideshoots to leave four or five leaves of fresh growth.

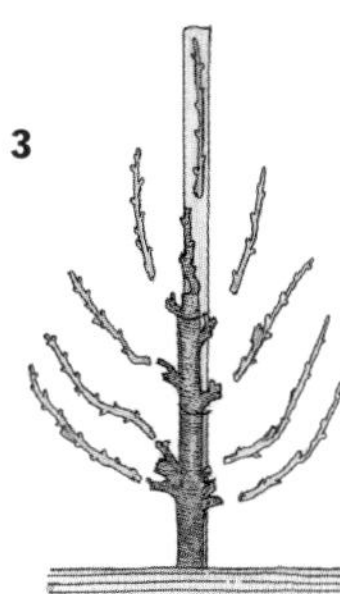

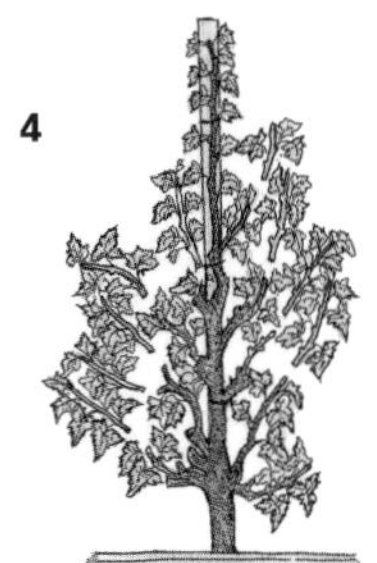

'Laxton's Giant' blackcurrants

Blackcurrants

My blackcurrant bushes have not been pruned for some years and are not bearing much fruit. What can I do?

It is important to cut out some of the wood each winter to get a steady supply of young growth. If the bush looks overgrown and has become unproductive, it is time to take more drastic action. You can either cut out about half of the old canes or reduce all the existing stems to the base, leaving one good bud on each. It will mean that there will be no fruit for the next season, but the bush should be flourishing by the next. If it is getting a bit old – more than ten years old, say – it might be a better to remove the bush and plant a new one.

Blackcurrant cultivars

Blackcurrants mature at different times:

- Early: 'Boskoop Giant' and 'Laxton's Giant'
- Mid-season: 'Ben Lomond', 'Ben More', 'Ben Nevis', 'Blacksmith' and 'Wellington XXX'
- Late: 'Baldwin', 'Ben Sarek' and 'Ben Tirran'
- Very late: 'Jet'

Jostaberry

Jostaberries (*Ribes × culverwellii*), a delicious cross between blackcurrants and gooseberries, can be pruned in exactly the same way as blackcurrants.

Are blackcurrants pruned in the same way as redcurrants?

No, they are not. Blackcurrants (*Ribes nigrum*) bear fruit on shoots that were produced during the previous year, and plants are pruned in order to remove old wood and to encourage the development of new, young shoots. Redcurrants (like whitecurrants and gooseberries), on the other hand, are grown so that they have a more permanent structure of stems, arising from a short, central stem.

Plant the young blackcurrant bush during its dormancy – that is, between autumn and early spring. At this point, although it may seem drastic, cut back all stems to just one bud above ground level. No pruning is required during the following winter unless there are any weak stems or ones that are low and droop along the soil. In the following year, cut out about one-third of the oldest stems and remove any low-growing shoots. Some gardeners cut back the remaining fruited stems to a vigorous new sideshoot; others prefer to leave them uncut. All gardeners, however, cut out any dead or diseased wood. Encourage new shoots to develop by applying a general fertilizer in spring.

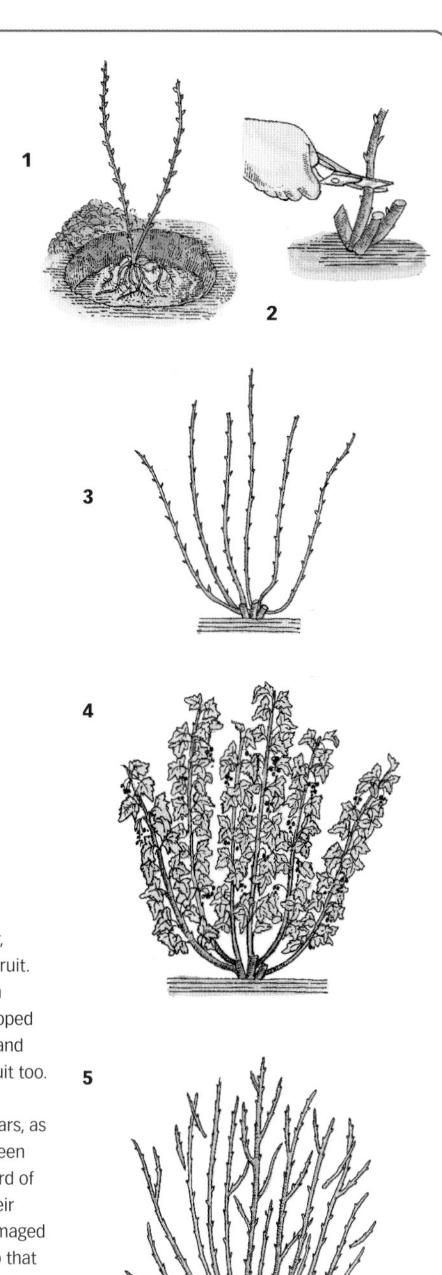

1 Plant young blackcurrant bushes in their dormant period, setting them slightly deeper than before; the old soil level mark will be visible on the stem.

2 Immediately cut back all stems to 2–3cm (1in) above soil level to encourage the development of fresh, young shoots from the plant's base.

3 By the end of the following summer, young shoots will have developed. No pruning is needed at this stage.

4 In the following year, these stems will bear fruit. At the same time fresh shoots will have developed from the bush's base, and these will later bear fruit too.

5 In all subsequent years, as soon as the fruit has been picked, cut out one-third of the oldest stems to their bases. Also cut out damaged and crossing shoots so that light and air can penetrate the bush.

Gooseberries

'Keepsake' gooseberries

Can gooseberries be grown in the same ornamental ways as redcurrants?
Yes, they can be trained as cordons, espaliers or fans. The red varieties look especially attractive trained this way. For cordons, plant the new bush and choose one strong leader and tie this in a vertical position to a cane. Reduce all sideshoots to one bud. The leader and sideshoots are reduced in this way every winter from now on. Once the cordon has reached its required height, cut back the leader to one bud each winter.

Espalier and fan gooseberries can be trained in the same way as redcurrants, but these are not particularly satisfactory ways of growing gooseberries, and the space is better used for other fruit.

Can gooseberries be grown as standard bushes?
Yes, they can. They are like conventional gooseberry bushes except that they are on a tall stem, up to 1.2m (4ft) high. The stem is usually a rootstock of *Ribes odoratum* or *R. divaricatum* onto which the gooseberry has been grafted. The stem will need to be well supported by a stake and tie. Once planted, prune as an ordinary gooseberry bush (see opposite). Remove any shoots that develop on the main stem.

There is an overgrown gooseberry bush in my new garden. What can I do to it?
The first priority is to open up the bush so that the centre is clear and the surrounding branches are thinned out. Cut out any suckering (straight) growth along with any low-growing and crossing branches. Tip back the new growth on all main shoots by about a half and cut back all sideshoots to one bud. After the first year, by which time it should have settled down, remove some of the older shoots to promote new growth.

Gooseberry cultivars
The season for gooseberries is from mid- to late summer, but cultivars have been developed to produce fruit at different times within that period.
- Early: 'Broom Girl', 'Golden Drop', 'May Duke' and 'Rokula'
- Mid-season: 'Bedford Red', 'Careless', 'Crown Bob', 'Green Gem', 'Invicta', 'Keepsake', 'Langley Gage', 'Leveller', 'Pax', 'Whinham's Industry' and 'Whitesmith'
- Late: 'Captivator', 'Howard's Lancer', 'Lancashire Lad', 'London', 'Lord Derby' and 'White Lion'

➡ Do gooseberry bushes need pruning?

Unfortunately, yes. I say 'unfortunately' because they are not the easiest of shrubs to tackle as they are covered with sharp spines. Remember to wear stout leather gloves and protect your arms.

The actual pruning of gooseberries (*Ribes uva-crispa* var. *reclinatum*) is similar in many ways to that of redcurrants (see pages 126–27). The pruning should begin in winter when the young bush is planted. Cut all shoots by about half, pruning back to an outward-facing bud. If there is a leader, remove it back to the first sideshoot. In the following winter, cut back all main stems to about half. Choose some stronger-growing, well-placed sideshoots that come from these main stems and cut these back to half their length. Cut all remaining sideshoots back to one bud so they are about 5cm (2in) long. In the following and subsequent winters, cut all main shoots back to about a half of the new growth, and cut all sideshoots from these back to one bud or about 5cm (2in) long. Also remove any low-growing growth and one or two older stems from the centre so that the middle of the bush stays open. Some gardeners also like to prune some of the sideshoots (but not the main shoots) back to about 10cm (4in) in summer to make it easier to pick the fruit.

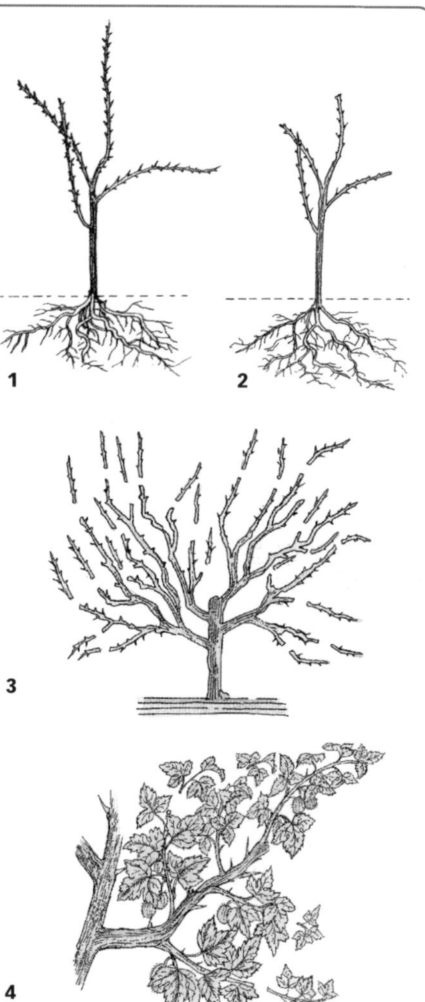

1 Plant a one-year-old gooseberry between late autumn and late winter. Set the plant firmly in the soil, only fractionally deeper than before, making sure it has a 'leg'.

2 Prune back each main branch by half, cutting to an upward-pointing bud. Make sure that the plant has a stem 15–20cm (6–8in) long.

3 By late autumn or early winter of the following year, strong shoots will have developed. Shorten them by a half to inward- and upward-pointing buds. In the following late autumn, shorten all leading shoots by a half. Shorten laterals to 5cm (2in) long and cut out crossing shoots.

4 In subsequent years in summer, prune lateral shoots produced that season to five leaves. Do not prune leading shoots. In the following winter, cut back leading shoots by half and all lateral shoots to about two buds from their base.

Raspberries

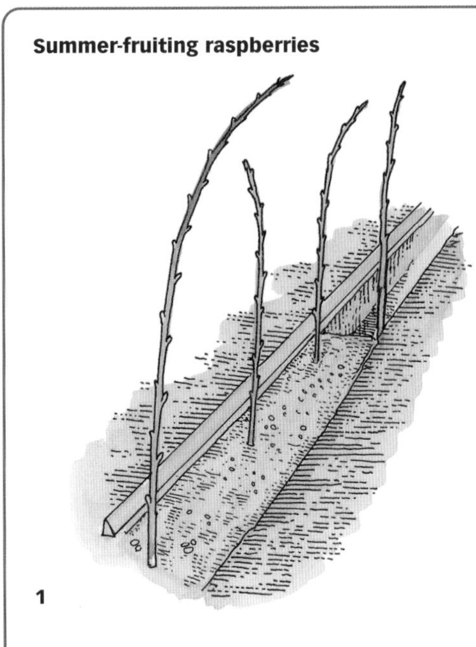

Summer-fruiting raspberries

Raspberries

A lot of my summer-fruiting raspberry canes seem to have died. What has gone wrong?

Raspberry (*Rubus idaeus*) canes naturally die back after fruiting. Fortunately, by the time this happens a new set of canes has been formed, and pruning raspberries largely consists of removing these old, dead canes.

Plant new canes in winter, whenever the ground is not frozen or waterlogged, setting them in a row about 45cm (18in) apart. Cut each cane down to 25–30cm (10–12in) from the ground. In the following spring, the new growth will have started and the stumps of the old canes can be cut off at the base. As the canes grow, they should be tied into a wire framework. These wires should be supported on stout posts set about 3m (10ft) apart. There should be three horizontal wires, the first about 75cm (30in) from the ground and the next two set at 40cm (16in) intervals. The wires should be as taut as possible. Tie the canes against the wires with soft string. Spread the canes out so they are evenly spaced along the wires and are not crossing over each other. They will not fruit in this first year. In the following late spring, cut out the tips about 15cm (6in) above the top wire. They will fruit in that summer.

Once the canes have finished fruiting, cut out the old canes at the base. During summer, new canes will have formed and these should be tied in as they grow to the wires. By the end of the year they should be taller than the top wire. Bend over the tops and tie this down to form a loop. At the end of winter, cut through these hoops about 15cm (6in) above the wire to a sound bud and remove the top of the cane. Fruit will appear again during summer and the pruning process is repeated.

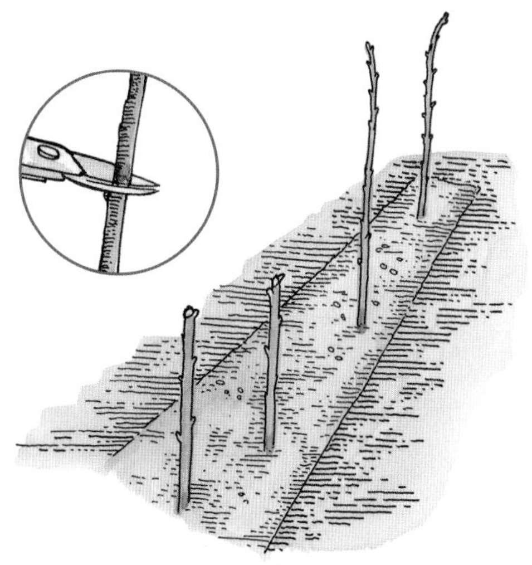

2

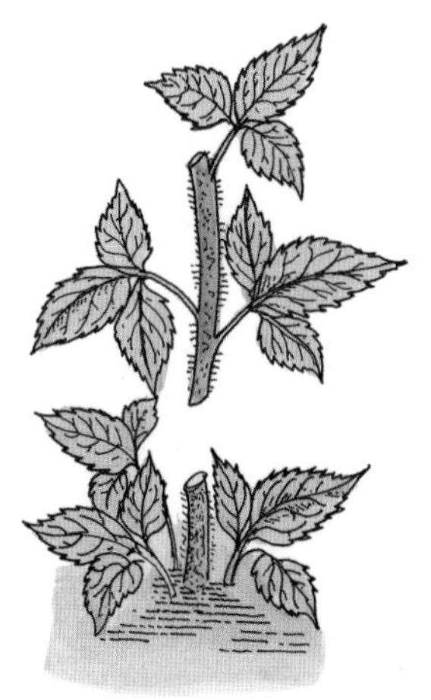

3

1 In winter, plant the canes 45cm (15in) apart and about 8cm (3in) deep. Align the rows north to south to ensure that one row is not excessively shaded by the next. If several rows are planted space them 1.8m (6ft) apart.

2 Cut them down to 25–30cm (10–12in) high just above a healthy, dormant bud. In late winter, re-firm soil around roots loosened by frost.

3 In spring, young shoots that appear from ground level will bear fruit in the following year. Cut off the old just above ground level. In the subsequent summer, space out the new canes and tie them to the supporting wires. Do not allow more than eight canes to develop.

4 In late winter, cut off the tips of all canes, about 15cm (6in) above the top wire and slightly above a healthy bud. In the following summer, fresh canes will develop that will produce fruit in the following year.

5 As soon as the fruits have been picked, cut down to their bases all the canes that produced fruit, leaving the young canes that developed earlier in the same year and that will produce fruit in the following season.

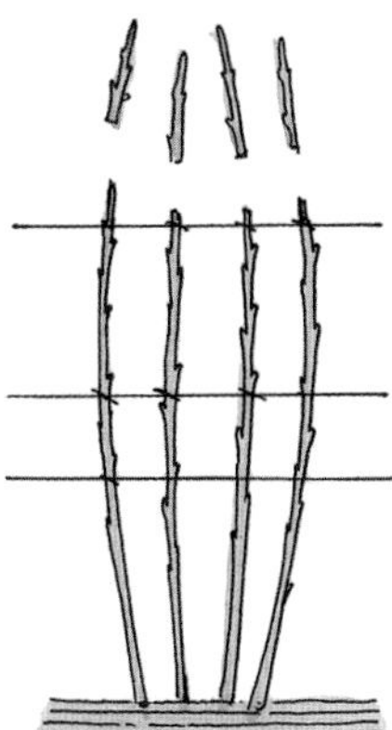

4

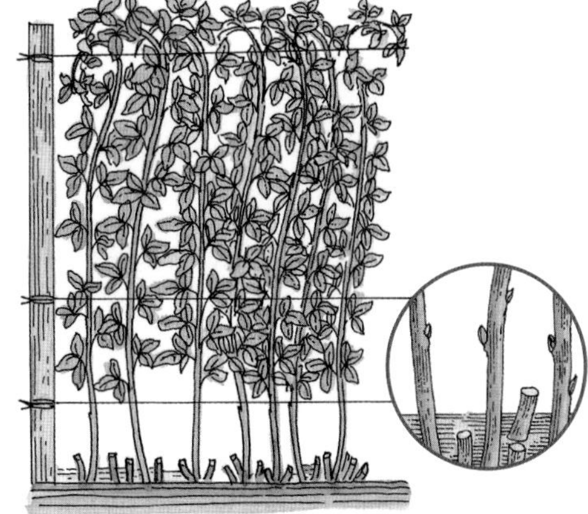

5

Picking raspberries

➡ Do I prune autumn-fruiting raspberries in the same way?

No. Autumn-fruiting raspberries fruit on the current year's growth and all the canes should be cut to the ground in late winter. The new set of canes will grow and should be tied in as they reach the top wire. Nothing more need be done to them (apart from harvesting the fruit) until they are cut down again at the end of the following winter, except to cut out the tips if they grow more than 15cm (6in) above the top wire.

➡ My raspberries are producing masses of canes and there is no room to tie them all into the wires. What should I do?

Raspberry canes are best spaced about 10cm (4in) apart on the wires. If necessary, remove some of the weaker canes from the base. Alternatively, if there are any canes that are shooting up from outside the row, dig these up and discard them.

Raspberry cultivars

Summer-fruiting raspberries include

- Early: 'Glen Cova' and 'Glen Moy'
- Mid-season: 'Malling Admiral' and 'Malling Jewel'
- Late: 'Leo'

Autumn-fruiting raspberries include 'Allgold', 'Autumn Bliss','Heritage', 'September' and 'Zeva'.

Autumn-fruiting raspberries

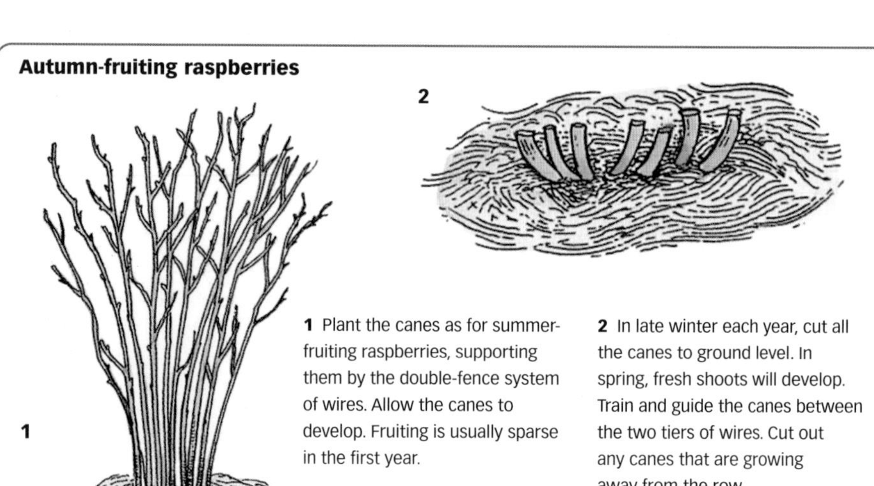

1 Plant the canes as for summer-fruiting raspberries, supporting them by the double-fence system of wires. Allow the canes to develop. Fruiting is usually sparse in the first year.

2 In late winter each year, cut all the canes to ground level. In spring, fresh shoots will develop. Train and guide the canes between the two tiers of wires. Cut out any canes that are growing away from the row.

Blackberries

Blackberries, hybrid berries and loganberries

I have tried growing a blackberry bush, but the long stems seem to go all over the place. How do I prune it?

Blackberries (*Rubus fruticosus*), although they are often called bushes, are really canes, rather like long raspberry canes. If they are left to their own devices they will grow all over the garden, with thorny stems whipping around in the wind, tearing at other plants and even people. The best way to control them is to tie them into wires, which should be supported on posts spaced about 3m (10ft) apart. Use four strong wires with about 30cm (12in) between each one, the lowest being about 75cm (30in) from the ground. The young plants are planted in winter, with vigorous cultivars spaced about 5m (16ft) apart, and less vigorous forms about 3m (10ft) apart. Cut back the stem of the new plant to about 25cm (10in).

Hybrid berries

Boysenberries, tayberries and loganberries are examples of hybrid berries, and these are pruned and trained in the same way as blackberries. Indeed, they can even share the same wirework, with a blackberry at one end and a hybrid berry at the other.

Loganberries

Weaving method

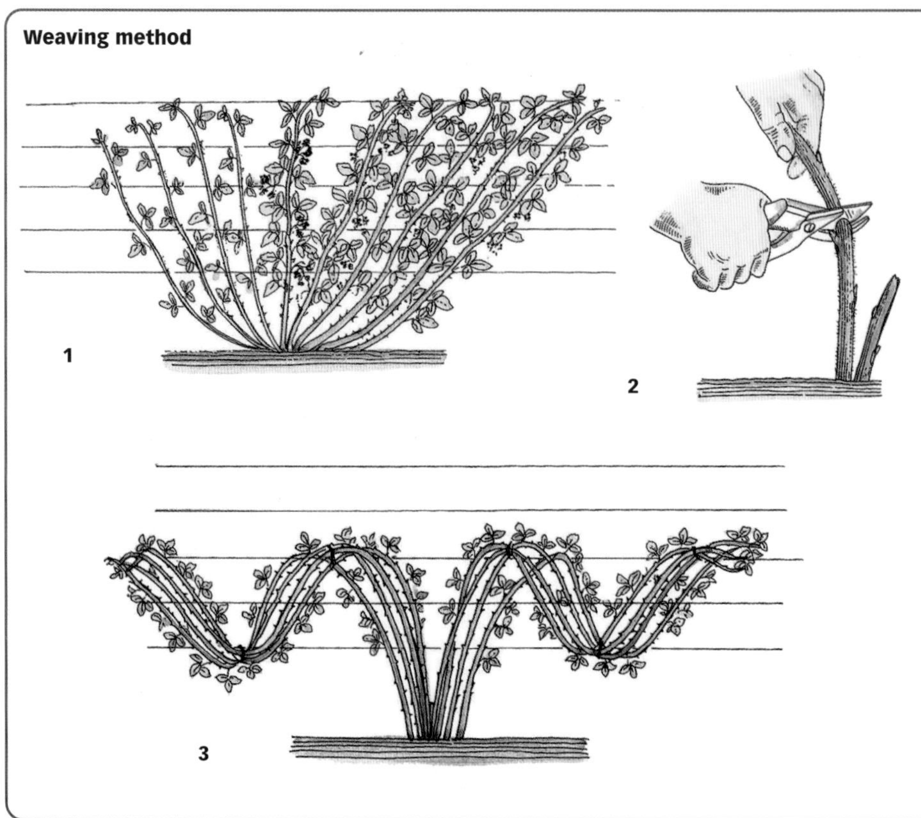

There are several ways of training the canes. Blackberries are the same as raspberries in that once the cane has fruited it dies, and at the same time new canes will have grown throughout the summer to replace them. The most popular way to train the bush is to fan out the individual canes on either side of the plant and tie each one to the wire. The new canes grow up through the middle, between the sets of canes. As soon as fruiting is over, the old canes are cut out at the base and the new ones are trained into their place.

An alternative method is to tie all the fruiting canes to one side and tie in all the new canes as they develop to the other side. Once fruiting is over, all the old canes are cut out and the new canes that develop the following year are tied in their place and so on. This method is better if the bush is situated in an exposed position, because the new canes are tied in as they develop and not left to blow around. However, it does take up a lot more space and is not suitable for a small garden.

Another similar system, known as roping, involves tying the canes in groups of three or four to individual wires, and this is an easier and quicker system of training cane fruits than the fan method. Training the old and new canes on different sides of the plant makes pruning easier. Old fruited canes are cut off at their bases. In the following season, young canes will develop on the other side, and these are trained in small groups along the wires.

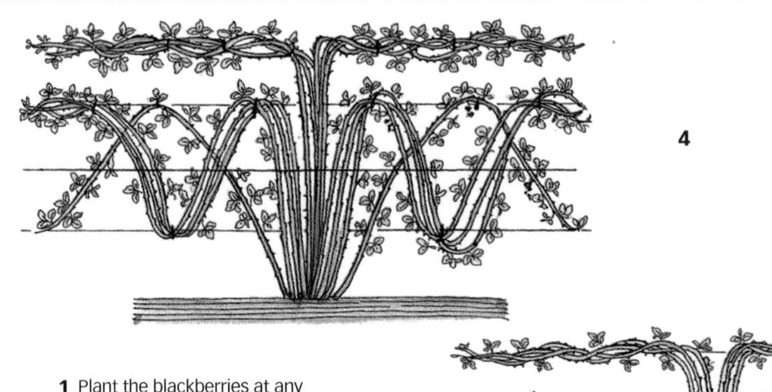

5

1 Plant the blackberries at any time from mid-autumn to late winter, positioning the young plants 1.8–3m (6–10ft) apart against a series of horizontal supporting wires. Each year the plants will produce young canes that bear fruit in the following season.

2 Cut down each stem to about 23cm (9in) above the ground, severing just above a healthy bud to encourage the development of young shoots from ground level. In early spring, firm soil over the plant's roots; severe frosts often disturb the soil, which can retard the bush's growth.

3 In the first summer, young canes grow from the plant's base. Weave and secure them between the lower three tiers of wires, spreading them equally on both sides. At this stage, the top wires are bare, so that young canes produced in the following year can be trained along them.

4 In the following year, train in the new canes that developed from the plant's base, guiding them straight up and then in both directions along the top wire or wires. Loosely tie them in clusters so that air and light can penetrate among them. Do not allow the two seasons' canes to become mixed, because this will create problems later in the year.

5 The old canes will start to bear fruit in late summer. As soon as fruiting is over, cut out to their bases all those canes that produced fruit. Sever the ties that secure them to the wires and burn both the ties and the old canes.

6 When the old canes have been removed, untie from the top wire all the canes that were produced in the current year. These are the canes that will bear fruit in the following season. In autumn, cut off the tips from weak and young canes. In late winter, especially for plants growing in very cold and exposed areas, cut back the ends of shoots damaged by frost.

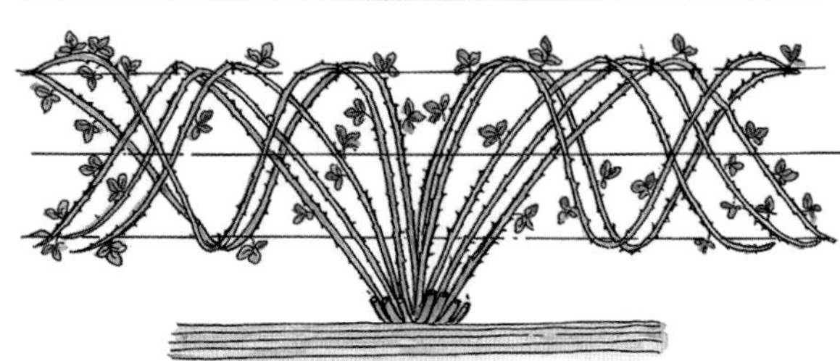

6

Blueberries, cranberries and kiwi fruit

➡ I have been thinking of growing blueberries. How should I prune them?
Blueberries (*Vaccinium corymbosum*) are not difficult to prune, especially during their first two or three years when no pruning is required other than to cut out dead or damaged stems. The fruit appears on old wood that is at least two or three years old, and so this should not be cut out. Once the plant is established, remove one or two of the older stems, preferably those that are no longer fruiting at the base, to help stimulate new, vigorous growth from the base. Also cut out any sideshoots that are no longer productive. If bushes are neglected and have become overcrowded with old wood, cut out all but a few young shoots.

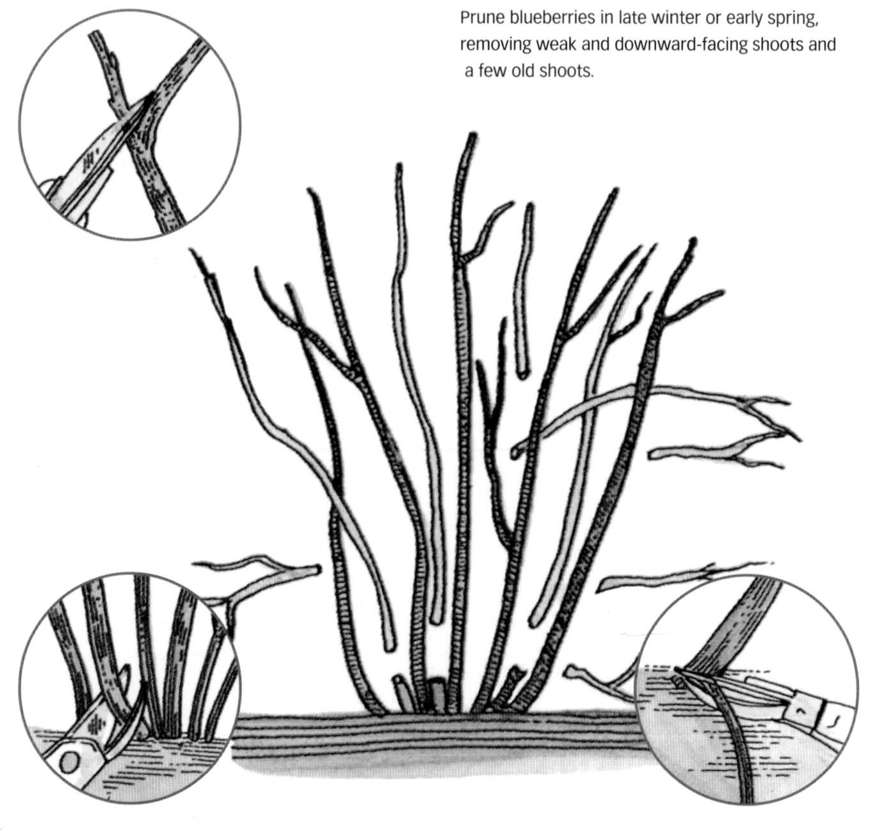

Prune blueberries in late winter or early spring, removing weak and downward-facing shoots and a few old shoots.

➡ Is it possible to grow cranberries in a garden?

Yes. Like blueberries, of which they are a close relative, cranberries (*Vaccinium oxycoccos*) are acid-loving plants that will thrive in borders as well as fruit beds. Plants need little pruning, other than occasionally cutting out very old stems in spring and making sure that they do not encroach on neighbouring plants. To keep plants bushy, use hand shears in mid-spring to snip off the ends of shoots. Rather than cutting off long shoots, they can be layered in autumn and encouraged to form roots. Sever rooted stems from the parent plant in the following autumn and replant them in spring.

➡ Can I grow kiwi fruit in my greenhouse?

Yes, but you will need a fair amount of space because they need to be grown against a system of parallel wires, similar to those used for growing raspberries. The fruits are borne on the climber *Actinidia deliciosa*, widely grown in temperate climates for its large leaves. In such regions, low temperatures and late spring frosts make growing this climber for its fruits difficult, but in warm areas or even grown against the protection of a warm wall it may be possible.

Because male and female flowers are borne on separate plants, it is necessary to plant one of each if you are to get fruits. Plants do not bear flowers for at least the first three years, and the fruits are usually smaller than those imported from warm countries.

Plant young specimens in spring, putting male and female plants next to each other so that they are practically entwined. Grow as espaliers. Cut each stem level with the bottom supporting wire immediately after planting. Allow two shoots to develop on each plant: one to grow vertically, the other to form an arm of the espalier. Repeat this training at each level of the espalier. Rub off unwanted buds on the main, vertical stems and between the horizontals. In late summer, pinch out the tips of the horizontal arms and shoots arising from them to encourage the development of fruiting spurs.

Kiwi fruit cultivars

The range of cultivars suitable for growing in temperate areas is limited, but one of the best is 'Hayward'. It is a late-flowering female form, with large, succulently flavoured fruits. Other cultivars include the female forms 'Abbott', 'Allison', 'Bruno', 'Montgomery', 'Saanichton' and 'Vincent'. 'Tomuri' is a male cultivar.

Blueberry cultivars

Blueberries need well-drained, acid soil. The following bear fruit over several weeks:

- Early: 'Bluecrop', Bluetta', 'Earliblue' and 'Patriot'
- Mid-season: 'Berkeley', 'Herbert', 'Ivanhoe' and 'Rancocas'
- Late: 'Coville', 'Darrow', 'Goldtraube 71' and 'Jersey'

Blueberries

'Miller's Burgundy' grapes

Indoor vines

How do I train and prune a cordon for dessert grapes?

Dessert grapes (*Vitis vinifera*) are usually grown on single cordons or on two or multiple cordons. The principle is the same for all, however. The vine is planted against a series of horizontal supporting wires, 30cm (12in) apart. The vines are planted at least 1.2m (4ft) apart if they are single cordons, or twice that if they are double cordons. The best place to grow them in cooler areas is against a sunny, sheltered wall, when the wires should be at least 10cm (4in) from the brickwork. In a greenhouse, the wires should be at least 23cm (9in) from the glass.

Plant a new vine in winter and immediately cut it back to two buds above the soil. In summer, select the strongest growth and tie that to a vertical cane. Cut back any other sideshoots (laterals) to five or six leaves. Any shoots (sub-laterals) that have formed on these sideshoots should be cut back to one leaf. In early winter, cut back the new growth on the leader by two-thirds. Cut back hard all laterals to a single bud. During the following summer (the second), again cut back any sideshoots to five or six leaves and any sub-laterals to one leaf. Any flowers that develop should be pinched out. During the next winter, again, cut back the new growth on the leader by two-thirds and all the sideshoots to one bud.

From this point, the vine is allowed to produce fruit. In summer, pinch out the weaker flower trusses so that there is only one truss per lateral. Prune all the sideshoots that are carrying fruit to two leaves beyond the flower truss. Any sideshoots that have no fruit should be cut back to the usual five to six leaves. Any sub-laterals should be cut back to one bud.

This routine is followed every year. Once the main stem has reach its desired maximum height, cut its new growth back to two buds each winter instead of the previous two-thirds. If the spurs get too crowded, remove some of them (see page 95–7).

How do I make a double or multiple cordon?

These are trained in the same way as ordinary cordons (see pages 142–43) except for the initial training. For a double cordon, two shoots are allowed to grow during the first summer, and these are trained horizontally instead of vertically. In the next winter, each of these is cut back to a vertical bud about 60cm (2ft) from the base. These buds will produce vertical shoots, and these are, in effect, single cordons and are treated as before.

For a multiple cordon, select two shoots to train horizontally and cut them back to 60cm (2ft) in the following winter, as before. This time, tie in the new main shoot horizontally. Next winter, again reduce the new growth on this shoot to 60cm (2ft). Now allow two sideshoots to grow vertically on each arm, each about 60cm (2ft) apart. Treat these four as single cordons from this point on.

Pruning a grape vine

Indoor grape cultivars

The following grapes can be grown in a greenhouse:

- Early: 'Buckland Sweetwater' (white), 'Madresfield Court' (black)
- Mid-season: 'Foster's Seedling' (white)
- Late: 'Alicante' (black), 'Gros Colmar' (black), 'Lady Downe's Seedling' (black), 'Muscat of Alexandria' (white), 'Mrs Pearson' (white), 'Mrs Pince's Black Muscat' (black), 'Schiava Grossa' (syn. 'Black Hamburgh'; black), 'Syrian' (white) and 'Trebbiano' (white)

Greenhouse grape vine

Single cordon grapes

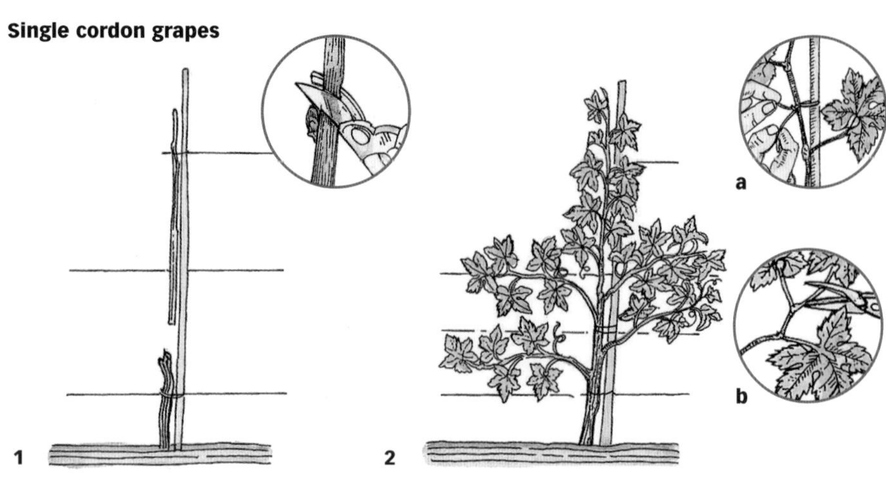

1 Immediately after planting, cut the main stem to slightly above a strong bud and about 50cm (20in) high. Prune all others to a single bud from their base. Tie the stem to a cane.

2 Train the central shoot upwards and tie it to a bamboo cane secured to the wires (**a**). In midsummer, use sharp secateurs to cut back all lateral shoots to just beyond five or six leaves. Cut back to just above one leaf all shoots that are growing from the laterals (**b**). In addition, totally cut back to the stem any shoots that are growing from the base of the main stem.

3 In the following winter, cut back all the lateral shoots (**a**) to leave just one strong bud at the base of young shoots produced in the previous year. At the same time, cut back the leading shoot (**b**), leaving only one-third of the previous season's growth.

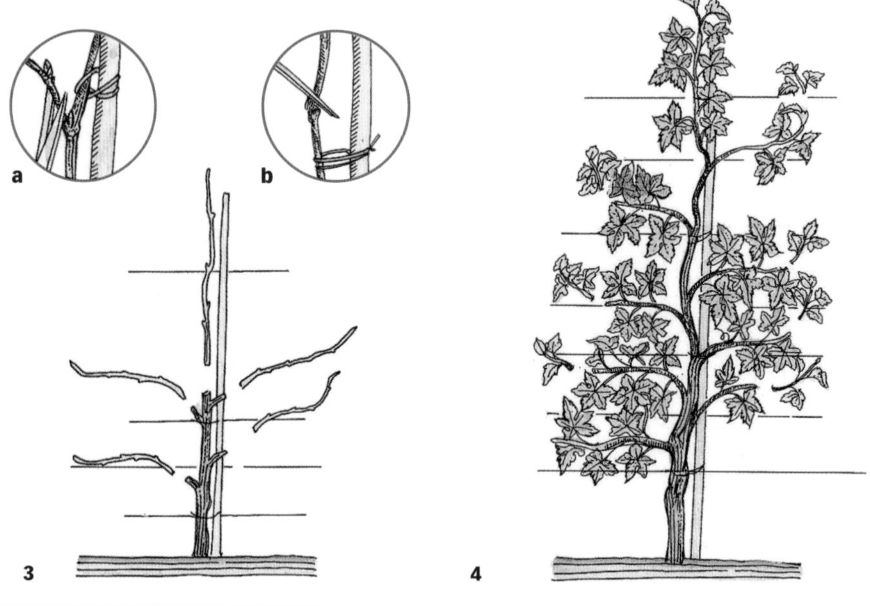

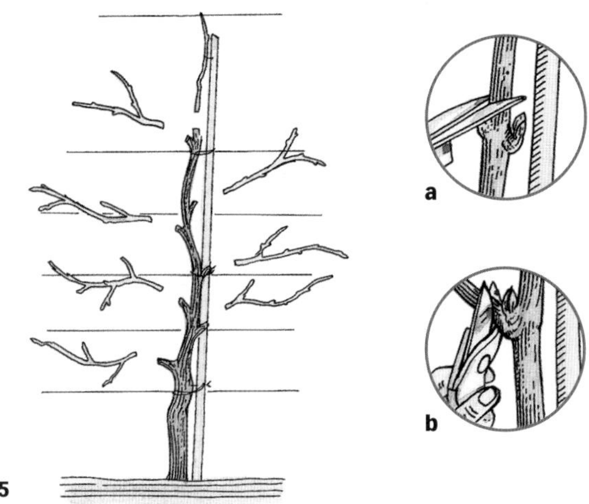

4 In summer, when the laterals have developed nine or ten leaves, cut them back to five or six leaves from their base. Pinch sub-laterals back to just above one leaf from their base. Pinch out flower trusses that form on the laterals.

5 Between early and midwinter, use sharp secateurs to cut back the leading shoot (**a**) to leave a third of the new growth from the previous summer. Sever the shoot just above a strong bud and cut back lateral shoots (**b**) to leave one bud on the new growth.

6 In the following summer, cut back laterals (**a**) that have a flower truss to two leaves beyond the fruiting cluster. Any laterals not bearing fruit should be pruned back to just beyond five or six leaves (**b**). If a lateral shoot is weak, do not let it develop more than one flower truss; pinch out all the others.

7 Between early and midwinter, prune the vine again. Prune lateral shoots by cutting them back (**a**) to the first strong bud on the growth produced in the previous year. If the leading shoot has not reached the top supporting wire, cut it back (**b**) to leave a third of the previous season's growth. When it reaches the top, cut it back to leave just two buds on the new growth.

a

b

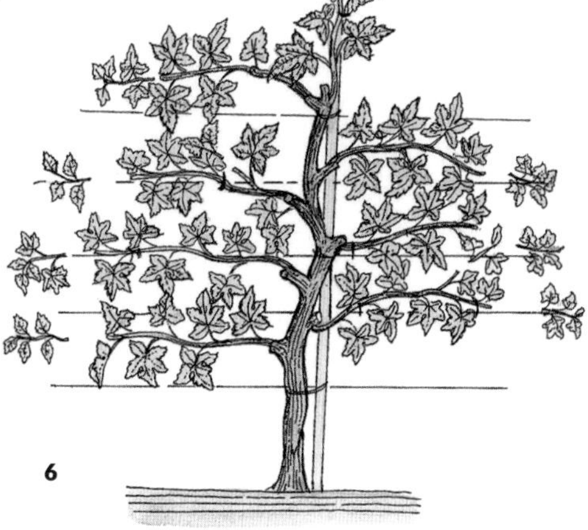

6

a

b

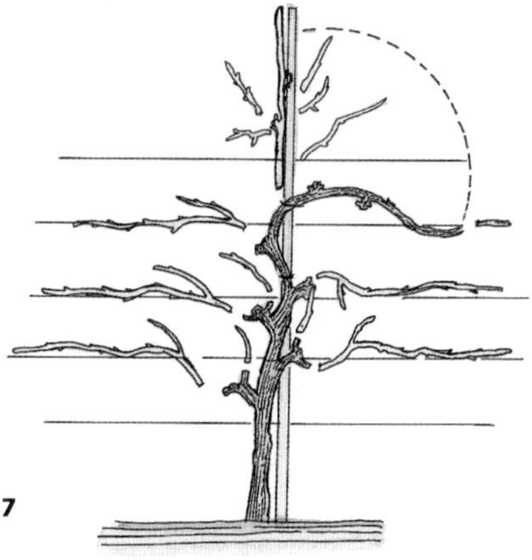

7

Outdoor vines

Is it possible to grow grape vines in a garden and, if so, how should I prune them?

It is perfectly possible to grow vines in a garden as long as the growing season is long and hot enough for the grapes to ripen. In colder areas, decorative vines can be grown, such as *Vitis* 'Brant', but the main point of grape vines is the grapes, and to get these it is important to prune

Outdoor grape vine

properly. Grape vines fruit on the current year's wood and unless they are thinned by the right amount the grapes will be too small or too late to be of any use.

There are several systems for pruning and training grapes – those for dessert grapes are designed to produce large, good-quality fruit, while those for wine grapes often concentrate on the production of a larger volume of smaller grapes. The most used method is a single cordon or a variation on it. The variations usually involve double or multiple cordons coming from the main rootstock. In cooler areas, dessert grapes are often grown under glass and these training systems are useful for both inside and outdoor culture. For wine grapes the most common is the double Guyot system (see below).

I have always want to try my hand at winemaking. How would I grow the vines?

A method known as the double Guyot is the most commonly practised method of training grapes for winemaking. A framework of horizontal wires is needed. The first wire is usually 40–45cm (16–18in) above the soil and the next three or four are set 30cm (12in) apart. Sometimes all the wires, apart from the bottom one, are doubled, to allow the new growth to be tucked between them rather than being tied in, which can be laborious if you have a lot of vines. A single-stemmed vine is planted in winter and cut back to two buds above the ground.

In the following summer, the strongest shoot is allowed to develop and is tied in vertically to a cane. Remove any other shoots back to one bud. In winter, cut back the new wood on the leader to 40–45cm (16–18in) from the ground, leaving three strong buds, two of which should be level with or just below the first wire and the third just above it. In summer, train all three of the ensuing shoots vertically, tying them loosely to the cane, and cut out any other shoots below them to one bud. In winter,

Outdoor grape cultivars

The following grapes can be grown outdoors, although late cultivars will ripen only in areas with reliably warm summers.

- Early: 'Madeleine Angevine' (white), 'Précoce de Malingre' (white) and 'Siegerrebe' (white)
- Mid-season: 'Müller-Thurgau' (white)
- Late: 'Chasselas' (white)

untie the three shoots and gently pull the lower two down until they can be tied on either side along the first wire. Reduce their length to 60–100cm (2–3ft). Reduce the length of the top shoot to three good buds.

That summer, fruiting shoots will rise vertically from the horizontal arms. If they are too numerous, prune them so that they are about 15–20cm (6–8cm) apart. Tie the remainder in and cut them back when they rise above the top wire, making the cut at least two leaves above the top bunch of fruit. Cut back any sideshoots that develop on them to 2–3cm (1in). Loosely tie in the three shoots that appear in the centre of the vine to the cane. As the fruit develops, remove some of the leaves to let in more light.

From this point on, the pruning is the same each year. Cut out completely the horizontals back to the main stem. Drop the lower two central shoots to replace them and, again, prune back the central one to three buds. In summer, repeat the action of the previous summer, and so on.

I have heard of the single Guyot system of pruning grapes. What is this?

This is the same as the double Guyot system except that only two instead of three shoots are allowed to develop. One is pulled down to the horizontal to produce the fruiting stems, while the other is shortened to provide the two buds for the following year. Other than that, it is exactly the same as the double system described above.

Thinning grapes

To ensure that individual grapes grow to a good size it is a good idea to thin the grape bunches. Start to thin the bunches as soon as the grapes swell. Over a period of a week or so, use long-pointed scissors to snip out any small fruits. As well as increasing the size of the fruits, this thinning encourages the circulation of air within the bunch and so prevents the onset of diseases such as mildew.

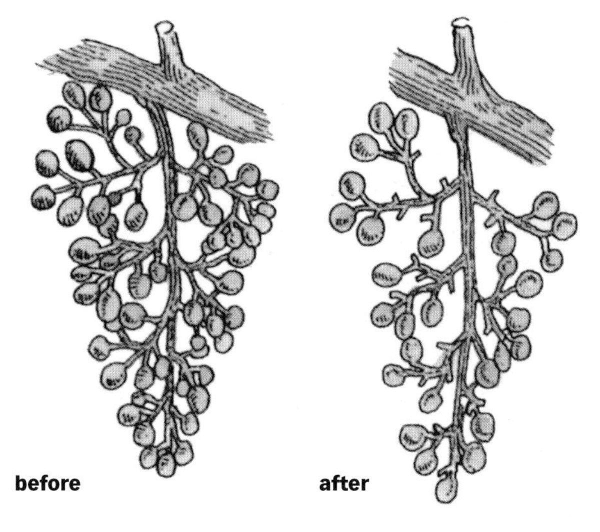

Troubleshooting

Old apple tree

I have inherited an old apple tree in my new garden. It is overgrown. What should I do?
Take a good look at the tree. If it is ancient with large areas of damaged or rotten wood, the best solution is to remove it altogether unless you want to keep it purely for its shade. On the other hand, if it just looks a bit of a mess with branches going in all directions, but is basically a sound tree, it can be pruned and brought back to a fruitful life.

As with all pruning, the first thing to do is to cut out all the dead wood; at the same time remove any branches that are diseased, dying or damaged. With this removed, the tree will already be opening up. Further improvements will be achieved by removing branches and shoots that cross back into the tree and any that rub against other branches. You should also remove any vertical shoots arising from the top of the branches (water shoots). Cut out any shoots that are overcrowded, so that light can get into the tree and air can circulate freely.

By now, the tree should be looking a bit more like it ought to, with an uncrowded, balanced, healthy branch structure. Further pruning can involve looking at the fruiting spurs and reducing them if they are overcrowded. It is often best to spread this kind of renovation over more than one winter. This is because, surprisingly perhaps, the harder you prune a tree the more vigorous it is likely to become, and the more vigorous the tree is in vegetative growth the less vigorous it is in fruit production. Once the tree has been re-established, continue to deal with it every year with your normal pruning routine (see pages 94–99).

I have just moved into a new house and the rose bushes in the garden are terribly overgrown. What can I do with them?

Irrespective of the type of rose, the first task is to cut out any dead, damaged or diseased wood. The next is to take out any thin or weak wood, any branches that cross through the centre of the plant and any that are rubbing against other stems. In most cases, it will also help to remove some of the older stems. If it is still overcrowded, remove a few more of the older or weakest stems. From this point on, prune as you would do for the individual types of roses (see pages 74–87).

I live in an exposed area, and trees are sometimes damaged by the wind. Is there any special pruning to help them recover?

The action you need to take will depend on the damage. In many instances, especially if you live near the sea, the most likely damage is that known as wind scorch, where the leaves turn brown or grey and become dry and withered. There is not much that can be done about this except to let nature take its course, but rest assured, the leaves will gradually be replaced.

Severe winds, however, can damage trees

I have an old mulberry in my garden and the branches almost seem to be breaking under their own weight?

As trees age, large branches often need to be supported so that their weight does not cause them to break and tear the bark, allowing pests and diseases to penetrate into the tree's tissues. Props are sometimes placed under them, or they can be held by cables suspended from branches higher up and threaded through giant, staple-like hooks, which are secured by washers and nuts.

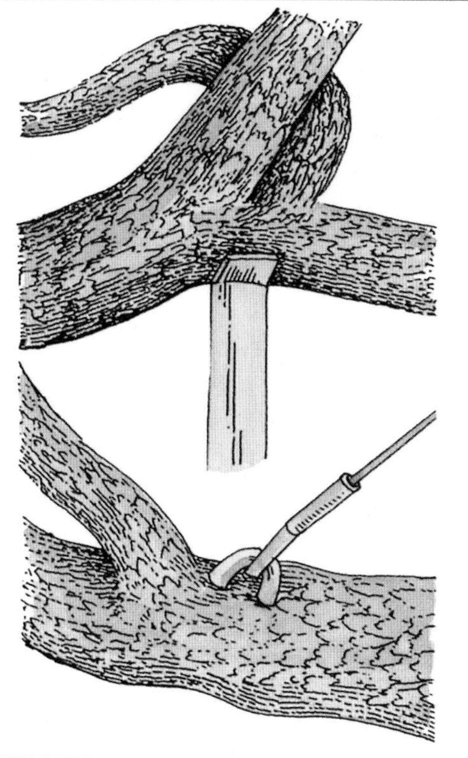

by breaking branches. Any broken branches should be completely removed, cutting them right back to the next branch. If the branch has been completely broken off, tidy up the wound, either by cutting back further to sound wood or by cleaning around the wound, removing loose wood and bark. Most wounds are left to themselves, and there is not much you can do to help if you cannot cut further back into sound wood. It is not normal practice now to paint wounds unless there is a particular chance of disease, such as silverleaf in plums.

We had a severe frost last winter which has killed shoots on some of my shrubs. What should I do?

Frost damage to rhododendron flowers

Frost damage of this nature is quite common when there are either severe frosts, which kill tender wood, or late frosts, which kill newly emerging wood. The stems are usually easy to see as they go brown, with the softer growth sometimes curling up. The way to cope with the problem is to prune back into sound wood, either to a healthy bud or to a junction with another branch or shoot. Although it may be time-consuming on a shrub with lots of burnt tips, you should prune out all such damaged growth.

Snow has weighed down some of the stems in my hedge, so they stick out sideways. Should I cut them out?

If possible, tie the stems back into the hedge, either to a stake or to other, sturdy stems. Protect the stems so that the rope or string does not dig into the tissue. If this does not work, you may have to take out the stems completely. These will usually regenerate, but there will be a problem with conifers, other than *Taxus* spp. (yew), which will not regrow.

It is better to avoid the problem altogether if you can. This can be done partly by pruning. Shape the top of the hedge into a point or slope so that most snow slides off. The other precaution is to knock off any heavy snowfall before damage occurs.

There was a lot of snow last winter, and it weighed down branches on some of my shrubs. Some were broken and others seem permanently bent. What can I do?

The broken or damaged stems should be cut back into sound wood, preferably back to a branch junction or where the stem joins another shoot. The stems that were pulled out of shape may be returned to their old position by tying them in, either to a stake or other branches.

In future, try to avoid these problems by knocking heavy falls of snow from trees and shrubs before damage occurs.

Snow-covered shrubs

➡ The leaves on my plum tree have turned silvery brown. What is wrong?
Plums are susceptible to a fungal disease known as silverleaf, which is a serious problem for all members of the Rosaceae family, although it mainly attacks plums (especially 'Victoria'), gages, damsons and cherries. Apples and pears are only occasionally affected.

Disease spores enter wounds, causing a silvery discoloration of the leaves. A purple fungus develops on the dead wood, and if affected stems are cut through a purplish-brown stain can be seen in the centre. Cut out all affected stems at least 15cm (6in) below the

Snowfall damage

Heavy snowfalls can damage hedges, by breaking and splaying shoots outwards. Instead of a square top (near right), cut a hedge with a rounded or sloping profile (centre and far right).

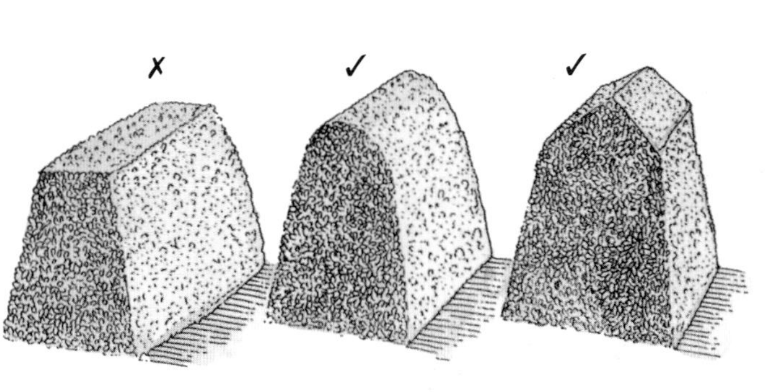

Silverleaf on a 'Victoria' plum tree

fungus. Paint the wounds with a tree paint that contains bitumen (available from garden centres), and water, feed and mulch the tree to encourage vigorous growth. Badly affected trees, with fungal bodies on the trunks, should be dug up and burned.

The following plants are particularly susceptible to silverleaf: *Cotoneaster* spp.; *Laburnum* spp.; *Populus* spp.; *Prunus* spp.; *Sorbus* spp.; *Syringa* spp.

What is die-back and what can I do about it?

Die-back occurs when the tips of a shoot are killed either by frost (see page 148) or by disease or some other agency. The problem is usually obvious because the tipsof the shoot turn brown and often stiffen. The shoots should be cut back to a strong bud or to a shoot that joins the parent branch.

I have heard that clematis can be pruned right back to ground level if they are affected by wilt. Is this true?

Yes, some large-flowered hybrids are affected by a fungal disease that causes the upper shoots of a clematis to wilt. Young leaves, and then the stalks, wilt and turn black. The problem is most prevalent in early spring and throughout the growing season. If you cut back the clematis to below ground level it should reshoot, and for this reason clematis should be planted 10–15cm (4–6in) deeper than the level in the original pot.

Before you cut your clematis to the ground, however, check that the problem is not caused by aphids or by slugs or snails. Remember, too, that clematis always grow better if they have their roots in moist, cool soil and the topgrowth in sun, so do not cut down your clematis if you suspect that the problem is caused because the roots are too hot.

➡ I have noticed that many of the shoots that I pruned last year have brown tips to them where the wood appears to have died. What did I do wrong?

The tips of shoots tend to die back if the pruning cut was made too far above a bud or from the point where it joins another stem. This dead piece of stem is known as a snag. The cut should either be just above a bud, sloping away from it, or close to the stem it joins, but not absolutely flush with it. See pages 18–20 for basic pruning cuts.

➡ Is it a good idea to paint pruning wounds?

In the past it was considered good practice to seal larger cuts with tar or special bituminous compounds, which were supposed to help healing and to prevent infection. This is generally not carried out now, partly because it has been found to be unnecessary, partly because trees recover just as well without it, and partly because it can sometimes cause problems of its own. Large wounds left when branches are removed from plum trees with silverleaf should be coated with a tree paint containing bitumen (see pages 149–150).

➡ My gooseberry suffers from mildew. Can pruning help with this?

Gooseberries can develop mildew because air cannot circulate freely through the bush. This can be improved by making certain that the bush has an open centre and that there are not too many drooping, lower branches, which not only make the fruit dirty but also impede the air circulation (see pages 130–1). When you are replacing the bushes, plant resistant cultivars, such as 'Invicta' or 'Lancashire Lad'.

Spreading disease

In addition to keeping your pruning tools clean and sharp, it is worth using a sterilant such as tri-sodium orthophosphate on your secateurs and pruning saw, especially if you have been cutting back plants that are diseased or that you suspect may be diseased.

Unpainted saw cut

Glossary

bark-ringing
Removing a narrow section of bark from the trunk of apple trees, carried out to slow down the growth of trees that are too vigorous.

biennial bearing
A term for when fruit trees bear a heavier crop in one year than the next.

brutting
Way of pruning cobnuts (*Corylus avellana*) where the main sideshoots are broken, not cut, about half-way along and allowed to hang down.

bullace
A type of small plum tree.

bush tree
A tree with a short trunk and many branches.

climber
A plant that needs support from another plant or structure such as a wall or fence.

clipping over
Trimming a small amount of growth off the whole plant.

coppicing
The cutting back to ground level of a tree or shrub to encourage the growth of several new stems from a single rootstock.

cordon
A single-stemmed tree, tilted at an angle and restricted in height by vigorous pruning.

cutting back
The cutting down of a whole plant, usually a herbaceous perennial, to the ground when flowering is over. It is done to neaten the plant, but can encourage new foliage and even new flowers.

deadheading
A form of pruning, this is the removal of dead flowers and flowerheads. Deadheading neatens the plant and curtails seed production, which can encourage further flowering.

disbudding
Removal of flower buds from plants such as chrysanthemums, dahlias and tuberous begonias to promote finer flower display.

dormancy
Period, usually in winter, where the plant is alive but not actively growing.

dwarfing stock
The rootstock of a smaller-growing plant used to graft onto a normally larger plant to restrict its ultimate size.

eyes
A dormant growth bud.

espalier
Tree trained flat against a wall or wires so that it has one main vertical stem (leader) from which emerge a series of horizontal parallel branches.

fan
Decorative way of training a tree against a wall or fence with several branches radiating out in a fan-shape from a short main stem; the branches are in effect a series of cordons.

feathered maiden
A one-year-old tree that already has a number of sideshoots.

formative pruning
Pruning in the first few years to establish the basic shape and framework of the plant, for example an apple tree.

fruit spur
A shoot or short branch on which fruit is borne.

grafting
The top growth of a plant is artificially fused with the rootstock of another to form what eventually functions as one plant.

hard pruning
Severe cutting of all or most of the main stems. This usually encourages vigorous growth.

laterals
Side growth from a root or shoot. *See also* sideshoot.

maiden whip
A one-year-old tree that consists of a leader and no sideshoots.

multiple cordon
A cordon where two or three main stems, rather than just one, are allowed to grow parallel with each other.

new wood
Growth that was made in the current (or immediately previous, if plant is in its dormancy) growing season. It is usually still green and pliable.

nicking
Removing a small wedge of bark, a nick, just below a bud to prevent a branch from growing. *See also* notching.

notching
Removing a small wedge of bark, a notch, just above a bud to encourage a branch to grow. *See also* nicking.

old wood
Growth that was made before the previous growing season. It has usually hardened and is no longer green and pliable, but woody.

outward-facing bud
A bud on the side of the stem away from the centre of the tree or shrub.

pleaching
Pruning and training a tree in such a way that the branches reach out horizontally and link up with the horizontal branches of an adjacent tree to create a 'floating hedge'. The trunks are usually kept free of branches.

pollarding
Cutting back the branches of a tree to the trunk to promote the production of young shoots at the top of the trunk rather than from ground level as in coppicing.

pruning
The removal of dead, diseased and unwanted branches or shoots to rejuvenate the plant, aid production of good foliage, flowers and fruit, and keep it healthy and attractive.

renewal
Removal of older growth to be replaced by new growth over a period of a few years, rather than in one drastic pruning. Also sometimes known as renovation.

renewal pruning
Pruning technique used for tip-bearing fruit trees which leaves some sideshoots unpruned so that they can fruit.

reversion
When variegated plants produce a shoot of all-green foliage.

ripe wood
Mature, hardened wood.

root pruning
Removal of part of the root system of a fruit tree to promote fruiting.

rootstock
Plant used to provide the root system for a grafted plant.

rubbing out
Removing small buds by rubbing with your fingers.

sideshoot
Shoot growing out sideways from a stem.

snag
Brown, frayed shoot tip caused by the pruning cut being made too far above a bud or the point where it joins another stem.

spindle bush
A way of growing apples and pears in which the main growth is restricted to three or four branches. New branches are removed once they have fruited.

spur
Short sideshoots that end in a flowerbud and occur all along a shoot.

spur-bearer
Fruit tree that produces fruit on spurs along each branch.

spur-pruning
Pruning technique to encourage the regular development of spurs.

standard
A tree with a clear trunk beneath a head or crown of branches.

step-over
An espalier in which only the lowest tier is used.

stopping
Pruning the main stem of plants that grow from a single basal stem to make it bush out by forming sideshoots. Stopping makes the plant a better fuller shape and encourages it to flower more freely.

sub-lateral
Sideshoot from a lateral shoot.

suckers
New shoots growing from the base of a grafted tree or shrub.

thinning (fruit)
Removal of some fruit before it is ripe to improve the quality of the remaining crop.

tip-bearer
Fruit trees that produce fruit only on unpruned two-year-old shoots.

topiary
Regular pruning and training of certain trees or shrubs to achieve and maintain a desired shape.

water shoots
Clusters of shoots that appear on the trunk of a tree either from the base or from knots where branches have previously been removed.

Index

Page numbers in *italic* refer to the illustrations

A

Abelia floribunda 47
Abies concolor *22*
A. lasiocarpa 'Arizonica Compacta' 23
Acer 12, 39, 41
A. japonicum 'Vitifolium' *18*
A. negundo 'Variegatum' 32
A. pensylvanicum 'Erythrocladum' 28
A. platanoides 'Drummondii' 32
Ailanthus altissima 26, *26*
Alchemilla 12
A. mollis 13, *13*, 14
Allium 11
almond trees 124, *124*
Alnus incana 'Pendula' 27
Amelanchier 39
A. lamarckii 27, *27*
Ampelopsis 62
annuals 12, 13
cutting back 10
deadheading 13
apple trees *8*, 12, 88-9, *88*, *92*, *95*, *96*, 149
biennial bearing 96
bush apple trees 90
controlling growth 98-9, *98-9*
cordons 89, 100-1, *100-1*
dwarf pyramid trees 92
espaliers 102-3, *102-3*
fan-training 104-5, *104*
feathered maidens 90
formative pruning *91*
half-standards *90*
overgrown trees 146-7, *146*
renewal pruning 96
rootstocks 88, 89, 102
spindle bushes 92-3
spur-bearers 93, *93*
standard trees 90
step-overs 105, *105*
thinning fruit *105*
tip-bearers 93
tunnels 105
types of 88-9
Arbutus 39
A. unedo 39
arches, pear trees 89
ash trees 27, 28
Aster × *frikartii* 'Mönch' *9*
A. novi-belgii 9
Aucuba japonica 30, 33,34, *34*, *35*, 51, 53

B

bamboos 14
bark, winter colour 45
bark-ringing, fruit trees 98-9, *98*
bay trees 24, *24*, 58
bedding plants 13
beech 12, 49, *49*, 52, 53, 56
begonias 11
Berberis 30, 42, 47, 50-1
B. darwinii 53
B. gagnepainii var. *lanceifolia* 53
B. × *stenophylla* 47
B. thunbergii 'Rose Glow' *50*
Betula pendula 26-7
biennial bearing, fruit trees 96
birch trees 26-7
bird damage 113
blackberries 12, 135-6, *135-7*
blackcurrants 12, 128-9, *128-9*
blueberries 12, 138-9, *138*, *139*
Bougainvillea 60
box 12, 49, 58, *58*
boysenberries 135
branches
crossing branches 9, 21
removing 19, 20, *20*
supporting 147, *147*
Buddleja 12, 43
B. alternifolia 42
B. davidii 43-4, *43*, 45
B. globosa 39
B. 'Lochinch' 43
buds
disbudding 11
pruning cuts 18-19, *18*, 61, *75*, 151
bulbs, cutting leaves off 10-11
bullace trees 113
bullfinches 113
bush apple trees 90, 94
Buxus 49, 58, *58*
B. sempervirens 58

C

calendula 12
Calluna 37
Calocedrus decurrens 23
Camellia 14, 32
C. japonica 35, *35*
Campsis *61*, 62
C. × *tagliabuana* 19
Carpenteria californica 47
Carpinus 12, *29*, 52
C. betulus 28, 49, 51, 53, 56, *56*
Caryopteris × *clandonensis* 43, 47
Castanea sativa 28
Ceanothus 36, 43, 46, 47
C. arboreus 'Trewithen Blue' *46*
Cedrus deodara 'Aurea' 23
Ceratostigma plumbaginoides 43
C. willmottianum 43
Cercidiphyllum japonicum f. *pendulum* 27
Chaenomeles 42

C. × *superba* 47
Chamaecyparis lawsoniana 22, *22*, 23, 49, 54
C. nootkatensis 'Pendula' 27
C. obtusa 'Nana Gracilis' 23
cherry trees
fruit trees 12, 118-21, *118-21*, 149
ornamental cherries 15, 26
Chrysanthemum 10, 11
C. 'Hunstanton' *10*
Cistus 44
clematis 12, 19, 60, 66-71, *66-71*
Group 1 66-7, *67*
Group 2 68-9, *68*
Group 3 70
large-flowered 68, 69,70
late-flowering 61, 70
non-climbing clematis 69
seedheads 70
viticella clematis 71, *71*
wilt 150
Clerodendrum bungei 43
C. trichotomum 47
Clethra alnifolia 42
C. arborea 42
climbers 12, 60-73
clinging and tendril climbers 62-3
cutting to ground 19
twining and scrambling climbers 64-5
cobnuts 125
colour, winter 45
Colutea 39
conifers
hedges 33, 54-5
shrubs 31
trees 22-3
container plants 13
coppicing 28
cordons 95, 100-1, *101*
apple trees 89, 100-1, *100-1*
gooseberries 130
grapevines 140-1, *142-3*
multiple cordons 101
pears 89
redcurrants *127*
Cornus 12, *45*
C. alba 28
C.a. 'Sibirica' 45, *45*
C. alternifolia 39
C. kousa 39
C. stolonifera 28
Corylopsis 39, 42
Corylus 27, 28, 51
C. avellana 28, 30, 125
C.a. 'Contorta' 33, *33*
C. maxima 125
Cotinus 12, 45
Cotoneaster 42, 51, 150
cranberries 139
Crataegus 21, 30, 49, 51, 57
C. monogyna 56
C. oxyacantha 'Paul's Scarlet' *57*
crossing branches 9, 21
× *Cupressocyparis leylandii* 49, 51, 54, 55, *55*
Cupressus macrocarpa 55
C. sempervirens 'Swane's Gold' 23
Cytisus 42
C. battandieri 42

D

Daboecia 37
daffodils 10-11, 14
dahlias 11
damaged wood 9, 21, *40*
damsons 108, 111, *112, 112,* 149
Daphne 39
dead wood 9, 21
deadheading 14
annuals 13
herbaceous plants 10, 13
deciduous hedges 56-7
deciduous trees 25-7
Delphinium 12, 14
Deutzia 12, 42
Dianthus 11
die-back 150
disbudding 11
diseased wood 9, 21
diseases 149-50, 151
double Guyot method, grapevines 144-5
dwarf pyramid fruit trees 92

E

Elaeagnus 12, 30
E. pungens 51
E.p. 'Maculata' 32-3, *33*
elderberries 122, *122*
equipment 16, *17*
Erica 37
E. tetralix 37
Escallonia 47, 50-1
E. 'Donard Seedling' *47,* 53
E. 'Red Elf' 53
espaliers 95, 102-3, *102-3*
apple trees 89
gooseberries 130
pears *102*
redcurrants 127
Eucalyptus globulus 28
E. gunnii 24, *24,* 28
E. pauciflora 28
Euonymus 12
E. fortunei 'Emerald 'n' Gold' 32
Euphorbia amygdaloides 'Purpurea' 14
evergreens 10, 12
hedges 52-3
shrubs 31, 32-7
trees 24
Exochorda 42

F

Fagus 12, *49,* 52
F. sylvatica 49, 53, 56

F.s. 'Pendula' 27
Fallopia baldschuanica 19, 65, *65*
fan-training 104-5, *116-17*
apple trees 104-5, *104*
blackberries 136
cherry trees *118-21*
figs *123*
gooseberries 130
peaches 114-15, *115*
plum trees 112-13
redcurrants 127
feathered maiden trees 90
ferns 11
figs 122, *123*
filberts 125
flowers
flowering hedges 53
flowering shrubs 36-7, 40-4
see also deadheading
foliage
bulbs 10-11
large-leaved shrubs 34-5
reversion 32-3
shrubs 45
Forsythia 30, 42
F. × *intermedia* 'Lynwood' *42*
Fothergilla 39
Fraxinus 28
F. excelsior 'Pendula' 27
Fremontodendron 47
frost damage 148, *148,* 150
fruit, soft 126-45
fruit trees 12, 88-125
cordons 100-1, *100-1*
espaliers 102-3, *102-3*
fan-training 104-5, *116-17*
formative pruning 90-3, *91*
step-overs 105, *105*
thinning 105
Fuchsia 15, 43
fungal diseases 149-50

G

gages 108, 111, 113, 149
Gaultheria mucronata 30
Geranium 12, 14
gloves 16
gooseberries 130-1, *130-1,* 151
grapevines 140-5, *140-5*
greengages *108*
Guyot method, grapevines 144-5

H

half-standards, fruit trees 90, *90,* 94, *109*
Hamamelis mollis 40, *40*
hawthorn 12, 21, 49, 51, 56, 57, *57*
hazelnuts 125
heathers 37, *37*
Hebe 30, 37, 51
Hedera 58, 60, 62
H. canariensis 62
H. colchica 62
H. helix 62
H.h. 'Angularis Aurea'*62*
hedge-trimmers 16, *17,* 52, *53*
hedges 12, 48-57
conifers 33, 54-5
deciduous 56-7
evergreens 52-3
guides 48, *48*
snow damage 148, *149*
Helianthemum 44
Helleborus 15
H. orientalis 15
herbaceous plants 12, 13
cutting down 9, 10, 13, 15
deadheading 10, 13
Hibiscus syriacus 39
holly 12, 32, 33, 49, 51, 58
honey fungus 21
honeysuckle 12, 19, 60, 64, *64*
hops 60, 65, *65*
hornbeam 12, 28, *29,* 49,51, 52, 53, 56, *56*
Humulus lupulus 60, 65, *65*
hybrid berries 135
Hydrangea 44, *44*
H. anomala subsp. *petiolaris* 60, 62
H. macrophylla 42, 44,*44*
H. paniculata 43
Hypericum 51

I

Ilex 32, 49, 51, 58
I. × *altaclerensis* 'Golden King' *32*
I. aquifolium 'Pendula' 27
ivy 26, 58, 60, 62, *62*

J

Jasminum nudiflorum 46, *47,* 60
J. officinale 46, 60
Juniperus chinensis 'Obelisk' 23
J. communis 'Compressa' 23

K

Kerria japonica *31,* 31, *42*
kiwi fruit 139
kniphofias 15
knives 16
Kolkwitzia amabilis 42

L

Laburnum 150
ladders 16
Lamium 14
Lathyrus odoratus 11, 60
laurel 33, 34, 51, *52*
Laurus nobilis 24, *24, 58*
lavender 36-7, *36*, 49, 51, 53
lawson cypress 22, *22,* 23, 49, 54

leaders
removing 13
training trees 19
Leycesteria formosa 43
leyland cypress 49, 51, 54, 55, *55*
Ligustrum 49
L. ovalifolium 51, 52, *52,* 58
lilac 14, 39, 41
lime trees 26, 29
lobelia 12
loganberries 135, *135*
Lonicera 19, 60
L. nitida 49, 51, 52, 58
L. periclymenum 64, *64*
loppers 16, *17*
Lupinus (lupins) 12, 14

M

Magnolia 12, 39
M. grandiflora 46, 47
M. stellata 41-2
Mahonia aquifolium 32
medlars 107, *107*
Melissa officinalis 14
Michaelmas daisies 9, *9*, 15
mildew, gooseberries 151
mulberry trees 122, 147, *147*

N

Narcissus 'Jack Snipe' *10*
nectarines 114, *115*
Nepeta 13, 14
nicking and notching 99, *99*
nut trees 124-5

O

oak trees 12, 25-6, *25*
Olearia × *haastii* 30
onions, ornamental 11

P

Papaver orientale 14
Parthenocissus 62
P. henryana 62
P. quinquefolia 62
P. tricuspidata 62
Passiflora 19, 62
P. caerulea 60, *60,* 62
peaches 12, 114-15, *114-15*
pear trees 12, 88-9, *93, 94,* 98, 149
arches 89
cordons 89
espaliers *102*
rootstocks 102
varieties 93
pelargoniums 12
Perovskia 43
petunias 12
Philadelphus 12, 30, 42
Physocarpus opulifolius 39
P.o. 'Dart's Gold' 38, *38*
Picea glauca var. *albertiana* 23, *23*
Pieris japonica 'Variegata' 32
pinks 11
Pinus mugo 'Mops' 23
pleached trees 28, 29, *29*
plum trees 108-11, *110-11, 113*
bush plum trees 109, *109*
failure to fruit 113
fans 112-13
feathered maidens *108*
half-standards 108, *109*
overgrown trees 112
silverleaf 108, 148, 149-50, *150*
wounds 112
pollarding 28-9
Polystichum retrorsopaleaceum 11
poppies 12, 14
Populus (poplars) 26, 150
P. × *canadensis* 'Aurea' 28
P. × *jackii* 'Aurora' 28
Potentilla 51
P. fruticosa 31, 39, 42
privet 49, 51, 52, 58
pruning
cuts 18-19, *18*, 61, *75*, 151
disposing of prunings 17
reasons for 8
tools and equipment 16-17
when to prune 15
Prunus 15, 26, 150
P. glandulosa 42
P. laurocerasus 15, 30, 49, 51, *52*, 53
P. lusitanica 15, 30, 49, 53
P. × *subhirtella* 27
P. triloba 42
Pulmonaria 14
Pyracantha 47, 51
P. rogersiana 51
pyramids
dwarf pyramids 92
plum trees 110, *110-11*
Pyrus salicifolia 'Pendula' 27

Q

Quercus robur f. *pendula* 27
Q. rubra 25
quince trees 106, *106*, 107

R

raspberries 132-4, *132-4*
redcurrants 12, 126-7, *126-7*
renewal pruning, fruit trees 96
reversion 32-3
Rhododendron 12, 34-5, 51, *148*
R. ponticum 30
Rhus typhina 39
Ribes 42
R. sanguineum 42
rock roses 44
Romneya 43
roots
fig trees 122
pruning 94
rootstocks
apple trees 88, 89, 102

cherry trees 118
nectarines 115
peaches 115
pears 102
plums, gages and damsons 111
roping, blackberries 136
roses 12, 74-87
climbing roses 47, 84-6
floribundas 78-9
hedges 50-1
hybrid tea roses 78-9
miniature roses 76
overgrown roses 147
pillar roses 86
rambling roses 87
shrub roses 80-1
species roses 76-7
standard roses 82-3
suckers *75*
Rosmarinus officinalis 53
Rubus 42
R. cockburnianus 45
Russian vine 65, *65*

S

Salix 21, 45, 51
S. acutifolia 'Blue Streak' 28, 45
S. alba subsp. *vitellina* 28
S. babylonica var. *pekinensis* 'Tortuosa' 33
S. caprea 27, *27*
S. daphnoides 'Aglaia' 28, 45
S. 'Erythroflexuosa' 27, 28
S. fargesii 28
S. irrorata 28
S. × *rubens* 'Basfordiana' 45
Sambucus 45
Sanguisorba officinalis 9
Santolina chamaecyparissus 36, *36*
saws 16, *17*, 151
Schizophragma hydrangeoides 62
scorch, wind 147
secateurs 16, *17*, 151
security, wall shrubs 47
shears 16, 52, *53*
shredders 17
shrubs 30-47
conifers 31
deciduous shrubs 12, 38-44
evergreens 12, 31, 32-7
frost damage 148, *148*
fruiting shrubs 12
rejuvenating 30-1, *35*
snow damage 148-9
wall shrubs 46-7
when to prune 15
winter colour 45
silver birch 26-7
silverleaf 108, 148, 149-50, *150*
single Guyot method, grapevines 145
Skimmia 12
S. 'Rubella' *12*
snow damage 148-9, *149*
soft fruit 126-45
Solanum 19
Sorbus 12, 150
spindle bushes, apples 92-3
Spiraea 12, 42
S. 'Arguta' 51
S. japonica 'Goldflame' 32
spur-pruning, fruit trees 95, *95*, 97, *97*
standards
fruit trees 90, 94
half-standards 90, *90*, 94, *109*
roses 82-3
stems
brown tips 151
die-back 150
'stopping' 11
winter colour 45
step-over fruit trees 105, *105*
Stephanandra 42
'stopping' 11
stumps, removing 21
Styrax 39
suckers 9
quinces 107
roses *75*
shrubs 31
trees 26, *27*
sweet peas 11, 60
Symphoricarpos 42
Syringa 39, 41, 150

T

Tamarix ramosissima 51
Taxus 22-3, 49, 51, 54-5, 58, 59, 148
T. baccata *48*, *54*, 55, 58
tayberries 135
thinning
apples and pears 105, *105*
grapes *145*
Thuja 22
T. occidentalis 55, 58
T. orientalis 'Aurea Nana' 23
T. plicata 49, 54, 55, *55*
T.p. 'Hillieri' 23
Thunbergia 19
Tilia 26, 29
T. × *euchlora* 28
T. platyphyllos 28
tools 16, *17*, 151
topiary 12, 49, 58-9, *58-9*
training
climbers 61
step-over fruit trees 105, *105*
pear trees 89
pleached trees 29
roses 74
trees 19
see also cordons; espaliers; fan-training
tree of heaven 26, *26*

trees 18-29
- conifers 22-3
- coppicing 28-9
- deciduous trees 25-7
- evergreens 24
- fruit trees 88-125
- ornamental trees 12
- pleaching 28, 29, *29*
- pollarding 28-9
- reducing crown 21
- removing stumps 21
- training 19
- weeping trees 27
- wind damage 147-8

tunnels
- apple trees 105
- hornbeam *29*

V

variegated foliage 32-3

Viburnum 39
- *V. tinus* 30, *30*

vines 62-3, 140-5, *140-5*

Vitis 62-3
- *V.* 'Brant' 62, 144
- *V. coignetiae* 60, 62

W

wall shrubs 46-7

walls, damage by climbers 73

walnut trees 125, *125*

water shoots 20

weaving method, blackberries *136-7*

weeping standard roses 82-3

weeping trees 27

Weigela 30, 42, *42*
- *W. florida* 'Foliis Purpureis' *41*

whitecurrants 126

willow trees 21, 27, 28, 29, 45, 51

wilt, clematis 150

wind damage 147-8

wind scorch 147

Wisteria 12, 47, 60, 72-3, *72-3*

winter colour, bark 45

winter-flowering shrubs 40

winter pruning, fruit trees 94-5

witch hazel 40, *40*

wounds 148, 151, *151*

Y

yew 12
- hedges 12, 33, *48*, 49, *54*
- regeneration 23, 51, 54-5
- snow damage 148
- topiary 58, 59

ACKNOWLEDGEMENTS

Executive Editor: **Emily van Eesteren**
Editor: **Rachel Lawrence**
Executive Art Editor: **Peter Burt**
Designer: **Stephen Carey**
Production Controller: **Ian Paton**
Picture Research: **Charlotte Deane**

Photography in Source Order

Eric Crichton 2, 7 top, 57, 64, 76 bottom, 82, 94, 96 bottom, 104, 105, 107, 108 top, 112, 114, 115, 118, 124, 125, 128, 135 top, 135 bottom

Garden Picture Library/Mark Bolton 29
/Christopher Gallagher 8
/John Glover 58 top, 62
/Howard Rice 39
/J.S. Sira 148
/Nigel Temple 4-5, 102
/Mel Watson 47 top

John Glover 31, 113

Harpur Garden Library 25, 26, 33 top, 52 bottom, 61, 84, 90, 93, 110, 130
/Home Farm Balscote 72

Andrew Lawson 22 top, 24 top, 27 bottom, 36, 42, 50, 52 top, 58 bottom, 60, 76 top, 78, 88, 95, 134, 141 top, 151

S & O Mathews 7 bottom, 21, 34, 43, 46, 56, 69, 70 top, 85, 106, 122, 140, 146, 149

Clive Nichols 13, 18, 45
/The Nichols Garden, Reading 24 bottom
/White Windows, Hampshire 33 bottom

Octopus Publishing Group Limited 11, 22 bottom, 35, 38, 55 left, 74, 81 top, 81 bottom
/Mark Bolton 6, 15, 23, 30, 144
/Jerry Harpur 9, 10 top, 10 bottom, 37, 49, 73, 98
/Neil Holmes 132, 139, 141 bottom
/Sean Myers 75
/Howard Rice 14, 27 top, 47 bottom, 100, 108 bottom, 150
/Guy Ryecart 17 top left, 17 bottom left, 17 top right above, 17 top right below, 17 bottom right above, 17 bottom right below
/Steve Wooster 32, 40, 41, 44, 48, 51, 54, 55 right, 92, 96 top
/George Wright 12, 66, 70 bottom, 120
/James Young 65